BOOK OF D

S. L. PERRIN

BOOK OF DEATHS

S. L. PERRIN

S. L. PERRIN

S. L. PERRIN

"Death is always on the way, but the fact that you don't know when it will arrive seems to take away from the finiteness of life. It's that terrible precision that we hate so much. But because we don't know, we get to think of life as an inexhaustible well. Yet everything happens a certain number of times, and a very small number, really. How many more times will you remember a certain afternoon of your childhood, some afternoon that's so deeply a part of your being that you can't even conceive of your life without it? Perhaps four or five times more. Perhaps not even. How many more times will you watch the full moon rise? Perhaps twenty. And yet it all seems limitless."

Paul Bowles, The Sheltering Sky.

CONTENTS

INTRODUCTION

Assuming room temperature, kicking the bucket, pushing up daisies, buying the farm, checking out, becoming worm food, going for a Burton, going home in a box, joining the choir invisible, popping your clogs, riding a pale horse, taking a dirt nap, shuffling off this mortal coil, in Abraham's bosom, giving up the ghost, the final curtain... To die.

If there's is one thing we all have in common regardless of race, colour or creed, then that thing is that we will all die... Yes even you reading this book right now. There's no escaping it, no point in worrying about it. So just enjoy your life as much as you can. However, nobody really knows exactly how or when they will die. We all hope it will be quietly in our sleep when we are much, much older but that's not always that way. Death comes in all sorts of shapes, sizes and flavours and that is what this book is all about, the never-ending work of the Grim Reaper and his many guises.

Taking a look at deaths from the bizarre, macabre, disturbing to pointless, questionable, deserved and even plain old funny deaths. BOOK OF DEATHS delves into numerous killers, victims and even accidents to look at just how/why people finally left this Earth. Some tales are pretty straight forward, while others are much more twisted and harder to comprehend. Some will shock you, some surprise, others will make you smile and there's even those that'll leave you questioning humanity itself. But, just remember this, each and every single yarn and the reasons behind the deaths in this book are 100% factual and that these are real stories, no matter how little sense they may or may not make. How stupid or unbelievable they may seem... All of them are completely true.

Now, sit back, relax and enjoy BOOK OF DEATHS.

CELEBRITY CAUSED DEATHS

Fame, fortune and adulation from millions of people around the world can be a powerful drug. Celebrity status can open a lot of doors, and yet be responsible for a lot of death too, sometimes accidental, sometimes on purpose. This chapter takes a look at deaths caused by various celebrities.

VENUS WILLIAMS

World-famous and highly respected, Venus Williams is one of the all-time greatest tennis players in recent years. She had been ranked number one by the Women's Tennis Association, Venus has won four Olympic gold medals and also been the victor in seven Grand Slam finals including the Wimbledon finals five times as well as fourteen (unbeaten) doubles titles. As I said, one of the all-time greats. In 2017, she also killed someone.

It was the 9th of June, 2017 when Venus Williams was driving through Palm Beach Gardens, Florida on a hot summer day. As she drove through an intersection, another car slammed into the side of her SUV, T-boning it at speed. The other car that hit Williams was being driven by Linda Barson, who actually survived the accident. But her husband Jerome, aged 78, was not so lucky. Suffering from multiple serious head injuries, Jerome was taken to hospital, but he died just two weeks later on the 23rd of June. Initial reports blamed Williams for the accident stating that she tried to speed through the intersection when she didn't have right of way and for a while, Williams was vindicated for the crime. But a later investigation and CCTV footage showed that another car had actually cut her off by making an illegal left turn. So Venus Williams had entered the intersection legally, but when the other car cut her off, she had to unexpectedly slow down and that was when the fatal crash happened that eventually killed Jerome Barson. The Barson family raised a case against the Palm Beach government for the accidental death of Jerome, blaming inadequate signs for the crash… Though this case was only raised after the family tried and failed to blame Venus Williams for the crash initially.

BRUCE/CAITLYN JENNER

Quite easily the world's most famous transgender person on the planet. But before becoming known around the globe as Caitlyn Jenner, she was known as Bruce Jenner and he was an Olympic gold medal-winning decathlete in 1976. An all American hero loved by millions. Even before the Olympics, Bruce had a very successful career in athletics, he won the French national championship in 1975 as well as securing a gold medal at the Pan American Games in the same year. He also broke several tournament records though his athletic life and even went on to have a semi-successful TV and movie career after retiring from sports. In 1991, Bruce married Kris Kardashian and helped kick-start the celebrity cancer that is the Kardashians. But, helping create the Kardashians (as unpleasant as they are) is still insignificant compared to killing someone.

Bruce Jenner began to transition into Caitlyn in 2015 when he admitted to being a trans-woman during an interview with Diane Sawyer. It was also in 2015 when he killed someone, four months before that interview. Bruce was driving his SUV along the Pacific Coast Highway in Malibu, California on the 7th of February, when he rear-ended a car being driven by retired actress Kim Howe, 69. Now, reports on exactly what happened vary, but the most common story of events seem to state that a car came to a sudden stop on the highway, behind that car was Howe driving a white Lexus and she had to brake suddenly. This was when the SUV being driven by Jenner smashed into the Lexus being driven by Kim Howe. The force of the crash pushed Howe's car into the opposite lane of the highway where it was hit by a fast-approaching black Hummer and that crashed caused Kim Howe to die via the impact. Bruce Jenner offered a voluntary blood sample and sobriety test, both of which proved to be negative, reports claim that he was not speeding at the time either. Prosecutors ultimately declined to press charges against Bruce Jenner for his involvement in the crash, though the stepchildren of the victim, Kim Howe, did blame Jenner for the crash claiming the hormone pills that Bruce Jenner was taking as he transitioned into Caitlyn in 2015 hindered his driving ability. Despite the claims and attempt to blame Bruce/Caitlyn for the death, no charges were ever brought against the star.

BOOK OF DEATHS

MATTHEW BRODERICK

In the mid-eighties, Matthew Broderick was forging a career in the movies and really making a name for himself as a big Hollywood star too. In 1986, he starred in the comedy smash hit *Ferris Bueller's Day Off* playing the titular Ferris Bueller. Alongside him in the film was Jennifer Grey, and the two became a couple while shooting the movie. It was while Grey was promoting her new film, *Dirty Dancing* in the UK when death occurred.

Deciding to mix the film's promotion with a short holiday, both Broderick and Grey toured Northern Ireland by car. Matthew Broderick rented out and drove a BMW 316. The couple set out from Irvinestown on the 5th of August, 1987, driving towards the small town of Maguiresbridge. It was around 3:00 PM in the afternoon when Broderick pulled into a garage near Enniskillen to ask for directions and this was where an off-duty policeman offered to drive ahead and show them the best route, Broderick declined the kind offer. Instead, he chose to find his own way to Maguiresbridge and set off again. Just a few miles into the drive and it began to rain heavily. Once more, Matthew Broderick found a garage and pulled in, the rain stopped and he and Jennifer Grey continued their Northern Ireland tour heading back out onto the open country roads. The details on exactly what happened next are mostly unknown, but it is widely believed that American Matthew Broderick momentarily forgot he was in the UK and began driving on the wrong side of the road.

It was less than a mile down the road when the BMW being driven by Broderick had a head-on collision with a Volvo driven by Anna Gallagher, 28 along with her passenger and mother, Margaret Doherty, 63. Both Matthew Broderick and Jennifer Grey suffered multiple, various injures including several cuts and bruises, a broken leg and ribs, concussion, a collapsed lung and whiplash. However, their numerous injures were relatively tame compared to those of the daughter and her mother who were rushed to a hospital, only for both to die of their injuries later. Even today, Matthew Broderick claims to have no knowledge of what happened, when interviewed by reporters outside of the hospital at the time, he reportedly said:

"I don't remember the day. I don't remember even getting up in the morning. I don't remember making my bed. What I first remember is waking up in the hospital, with a very strange feeling going on in my leg."

Originally, Matthew Broderick was charged with death by dangerous driving and faced up to ten years in prison... But those charges were later reduced to the much lesser charge of careless driving and he was fined just £140... For accidentally killing two people. I'll leave you to make your own judgements on that ruling.

DON KING

Boxing is a very brutal sport. Some call it majestic and gladiatorial, others, barbaric. Either way, it can't be disputed that when it came to boxing promotion, nobody did it bigger or better than Don King. He is the man behind some of the biggest and most famous boxing matches in history (the famed 1974, *Rumble in the Jungle* between Muhammad Ali and George Foreman to name just one), often pitting the best of the best against each other. But he had a bit of a shady and questionable side too. Don King was often the centre of many controversies running through the sport of boxing and he's even been (allegedly) connected to organized crime, in particular his relationship with the infamous mob boss, John Gotti. Oh yeah, King is also known to have killed two people.

In the 1950s, way before Don King became a boxing promoter, he ran a few not entirely 'legal' gambling houses and various other betting schemes, which made him a lot of money. So much so that he dropped out of university so he could concentrate on his racketeering. It was on the 12th of December, 1954 when King caught Hillary Brown attempting to rob one of his gambling houses. Don King shot Brown in the back, killing him and the incident was ruled as justifiable homicide, meaning he didn't face a jail sentence.

The second murder was not quite as justifiable. Don King served three years and eleven months for, what was ruled as the non-negligent manslaughter of Sam Garrett. It was the 20th of April, 1966 when King spotted Garret at a bar. Now, Sam Garret supposedly owed Don King more than $600 over a bet and King obviously wanted his money back.

BOOK OF DEATHS

The pair began to argue in the bar before a full-on fight broke out which then spilt out into the street. The fight became very bloody and brutal, at the end of which, Sam Garret was dead. Witnesses claim that Don King, armed with a gun, pistol-whipped Sam Garret, knocking him to the ground before repeatedly kicking him in the head and chest. The first police officer at the scene, Bob Tonne recalls that he saw:

"A man's head bouncing off the asphalt pavement like a rubber ball and another man standing over him with a gun in his right hand, applying another kick to the head."

The beating was so severe that it has been described by those who witnessed it as a 'demonic assault'. After serving his almost four-year sentence, Don King was later paroled in 1971, when he started his career in boxing by asking Muhammad Ali to compete in a charity exhibition fight to raise money for a Cleveland hospital. After that, King went on to become the most famous boxing promoter in history.

KEITH MOON

Famed for his very distinctive and even more so, anarchic and passionate drumming style, Keith Moon became known as the wildest member of rock band The Who... Which, if you know some of the legendary exploits of The Who, that's pretty damn wild. Keith Moon died in 1978 of an anti-alcoholism drug (heminevrin) overdose aged just 32, but in his short life, Moon managed to squeeze a lot in, not only becoming a legend and inspiration for so many musicians for decades, he also killed someone.

It was the 4th of January, 1970 and Keith Moon was attending the opening of a pub called The Red Lion in Hatfield, Hertfordshire which was owned by the son of one of his neighbours. As a favour (and for some free booze), Moon agreed to go to the pub and help raise its profile. I mean, who wouldn't want to go drinking in the same pub that world-famous rock star Keith Moon drank in? However, the publicity stunt had the complete opposite effect. The pub attracted very working-class punters and skinheads, very down to earth and grounded folk who perhaps were not really fans of the celebrity lifestyle. So when Keith Moon turned up with a small entourage in a chauffeur-driven Bentley, the locals didn't take too kindly to his rather audacious display of rock star wealth.

As the night went on, the fact Keith Moon refused to mingle with the other patrons by only talking to his own entourage, coupled with the fact he only ordered the most expensive brandy to drink (for free), attitudes toward The Who drummer began to sour. The locals, now drunk on cheap beer, began to get agitated with just how Moon was presenting himself. Last orders were called and the pub closed, Keith Moon and his friends left and climbed into their awaiting Bentley, driven by Moon's close friend, bodyguard and personal chauffeur, Neil Boland. But before they could drive away, several of the drunken pub customers surrounded the car, began to rock it and throw coins that bounced off the bodywork. So Keith Moon's bodyguard, Neil Boland did what he felt needed to be done, he got out of the car and confronted the gathered drunken pub patrons causing the trouble.

Panicking and in fear for his own safety and that of the others in the car, Moon jumped into the driver's seat and drove away from the scene. At this point, Keith Moon was seriously drunk and the fact he couldn't actually drive, not even when sober, meant he didn't notice that Boland was standing at a blind spot of the car trying to calm the situation down. As Moon drove away, Neil Boland was pulled under the car and dragged for around a hundred yards along the road, Boland's head had been crushed and he was later pronounced dead at the hospital. Keith Moon was cleared of the killing when it was ruled as accidental, but he did plead guilty to drunk driving and driving without a license or insurance.

Now, there have been a few conflicting reports as to just who was actually in the driving seat that night. Neil Boland's daughter believes that it was Keith Moon's wife, Kim who actually drove the car and accidentally killed her father. She believes that Moon just took the blame to protect his wife. However, Keith Moon's biographer, Tony Fletcher interviewed several witnesses that were there that night, including one of the passengers in the car that killed Neil Boland. That passenger was Jean Battye who confirmed it was indeed Keith Moon behind the wheel of the car that killed his friend and bodyguard Boland. A tragic accident that those close to Moon have said he never got over.

BOOK OF DEATHS

SID VICIOUS

From one infamously wild rock star to another. Sid Vicious was the bassist for pioneering punk rock band The Sex Pistols. It was while the band were at the height of their fame in 1977 when Vicious first met Nancy Spungen in London. The two quickly became a couple and entered a passionate but volatile relationship. The pair would argue and fight, but they still remained lovers. When The Sex Pistols broke up in January of 1978, Sid Vicious and Nancy Spungen stayed together and their relationship became even more destructive, especially when both of them become addicted to drugs, specifically heroin.

On the 12th of October, 1978, Nancy Spungen was found dead from a single stab wound to her abdomen in the hotel room in New York where she and Sid Vicious were staying. The only other person in the room was Vicious, so he was arrested and charged with the murder of his lover, Spungen. Sid Vicious was later released on bail. He changed his story several times and when interviewed by police at the time he reportedly said:

"I stabbed her, but I never meant to kill her."

However, Vicious also claimed he didn't actually remember anything at all about the night Spungen was killed too. Then, ten days after Nancy Spungen's death, Sid Vicious attempted suicide when he used a smashed light bulb to slit his own wrists, with many people seeing this act as one of guilt over the murder of his girlfriend. Vicious was taken to Bellevue Hospital, where he once more tried to kill himself by jumping from a window before being pulled back by hospital staff.

On the 2nd of February, 1979, Sid Vicious was found dead of a drugs overdose, his body was discovered by his mother. In a macabre twist, the overdose of drugs was one his own mother had been strongly suspected of giving to him. Sid's mother, Anne Beverley eventually admitted in an interview in 1996 that she did in fact kill her own son with drugs at his request because he was scared of going to prison over Nancy Spungen's murder. She also revealed that a note was found in Sid Vicious' leather jacket pocket after his death that read:

"We had a death pact, and I have to keep my half of the bargain. Please
bury me next to my baby. Bury me in my leather jacket, jeans and
motorcycle boots. Goodbye."

Obviously suggesting that Vicious and Spungen had entered some kind
of murder-suicide pact that night in the hotel, a pact that only half
worked out as planned.

There has been a lot of speculation over just who killed Nancy Spungen,
with several people believing that Sid Vicious was innocent all along.
But the general consensus is that it was indeed Vicious who killed his
lover, in a murder-suicide pact and that he was meant to die that same
night of a drugs overdose, the way he eventually died at the hands of his
own mother.

JAMES STEWART

One of the all-time greats, a true gentleman and a damn fine actor, one
of my personal favourites. James Stewart appeared in some of the most
classic films ever made, *Mr. Smith Goes to Washington*, *It's a Wonderful
Life*, *Harvey* and *Rear Window* to name just a few of his best flicks.
Known for his good looks and charismatic, magnetic personality. The
American Film Institute named James Stewart as the third greatest male
screen legend of the Golden Age of Hollywood. He was and still is
considered a cinematic legend, even after his death, in 1997... And he
killed multiple people too. But don't worry, these are no drink driving,
losing his temper, drug-induced killings. James Stewart was a war hero.
He began his acting career in 1932, starting in theatre productions before
moving into movies. In 1943, he enlisted in the United States Army as a
pilot, having already earned his private pilot certificate and commercial
pilot license.

James Stewart became the first American movie star to ever wear a
military uniform in World War II. During his time in the Army, he
became a Colonel and then Brigadier General in the United States Air
Force Reserve. Stewart also earned the Distinguished Flying Cross, the
Croix de Guerre and seven battle stars for his heroic work. He never
talked about his World War II career as he never felt comfortable killing
people as his experiences were very traumatic, so exactly how many

people James Stewart killed is unknown. But it is known he took part in several bombing missions as a pilot and played a hand in killing numerous enemy soldiers. Good looking, charming, a consummate actor and genuine war hero too.

HOWARD HUGHES

A hugely successful businessman, entrepreneur, industrialist, investor, engineer, also a highly skilled and record-setting pilot, film director and producer. Howard Hughes had many stings to his very large bow that helped him become a billionaire. As successful as Hughes was, he suffered from obsessive-compulsive disorder. Once one of the most famous and recognised people on the planet in his day, in his later years, he became a very strange recluse. Howard Hughes locked himself away in a Las Vegas hotel where he developed odd behaviour patterns. Sitting in a chair and watching notoriously bad movies on a continual loop while naked, he stopped bathing as well as refusing to cut his hair and nails among other bizarre behaviours before he died in 1976.

But before he went more than a little crazy, he killed someone. It was the 11th of July, 1936 and Howard Hughes was driving his car in Los Angeles when he hit and killed a pedestrian, Gabriel S. Meyer. After the incident, Hughes admitted that he had been drinking, but he was certified as sober at the hospital he was taken to after the incident. A witness to the accident stated that Howard Hughes had been driving very erratically and way too fast when he hit Meyer. The same witness also said that Meyer was not even in the road at the time and was actually standing in the safety zone of a streetcar (tram) stop when he was hit.

Howard Hughes was booked on suspicion of negligent homicide...Until his lawyer got involved. For some strange reason, the witness suddenly changed their previous story and stated that Hughes was driving perfectly normal and that it was Gabriel S. Meyer who was the one who had behaved erratically, claiming that he actually jumped out in front of the car. Due to the witness statement change, on the 16th of July, 1936, only five days after the death of Meyer, Howard Hughes was eventually found blameless at an inquiry into the death. Strange how a rich and powerful man was found to be blameless over a death when a witness changed their story after the involvement of a lawyer eh?

S. L. PERRIN

JOHNNY LEWIS

Johnny Lewis was a young and talented actor making a name for himself in TV and movies. He appeared in shows like *Malcolm in the Middle*, *The O.C.*, *Smallville*, *CSI: Crime Scene Investigation* and *Sons of Anarchy*. As well as movies such as *Aliens vs. Predator: Requiem* and *One Missed Call* among others. Lewis was not a major star, but he was an up and coming talent beginning to be noticed. In 2011, Johnny Lewis was involved in a high-speed motorcycle accident, in which he suffered severe head injuries. Lewis was offered an MRI scan, which he refused. His father pursued psychiatric treatment for his son believing the head injury was causing bizarre and illogical behavioural problems including mood swings and bursts of uncontrollable rage, once more Johnny refused the treatments.

On the 26th of September, 2012, Johnny Lewis was staying at the home of 81-year-old Catherine Davis, who ran The Writer's Villa in Hollywood. It was a kind of bed & breakfast for young and hungry talent wanting to make a name for themselves in Hollywood. Several now big names (Val Kilmer and George Clooney to name a few) had stayed at Catherine Davis' home at one time or another. On that day, Johnny Lewis randomly attacked a neighbour before jumping the fence and onto Catherine Davis' property. Now in the house that he was staying at, Lewis attacked and murdered Davis via blunt force trauma to the head and manual strangulation. Investigating police also found Jessie, Davis' pet cat dead. But Johnny Lewis never faced punishment for his heinous crime as, after killing his caring elderly landlady and her cat, he then climbed onto the roof of the house's garage where he fell (or jumped) to his death and was found by police, lying in the driveway. His death was ruled as accidental.

Johnny Lewis was known to have used and abused drugs in the past and it was first believed that he had suffered a drug-induced psychosis, which led him to kill. However, a toxicology report showed that he had no alcohol, drugs or any kind of medication in his body at the time of his death. He was 100% sober. It is believed that the untreated head trauma Lewis suffered after the motorcycle crash in 2011 may have contributed to the violent outburst which left Catherine Davis and her cat dead.

BOOK OF DEATHS

OSCAR PISTORIUS

When he was only eleven months old, Oscar Pistorius had both of his lower legs amputated due to a congenital defect. Even with his disability, Pistorius had a passion for sport including rugby, water polo and wrestling. It was in 2003 when Oscar Pistorius suffered a major knee injury while playing rugby. While recovering from the injury, he was introduced to running in 2004 which kick-started his successful career using specially designed running blades.

Oscar Pistorius took part in the 2004 Summer Paralympics and over the years he ran in both disabled and non-disabled contests. Along the way, he broke numerous records, but his greatest achievement came in 2012 when he took part in both the Paralympics and the Olympic Games. In fact, Oscar Pistorius was the first-ever amputee runner to compete at the Olympic Games.

By 2013, Oscar Pistorius was world-famous for his achievements and was thought of as one of the most influential people on the planet, earning the nickname of 'Blade Runner' due to his use of his carbon-fibre running blades. A hero to a great many. That same year he also murdered his girlfriend. It was the 14th of February, 2013 when Pistorius claimed he was woken in the early hours of the morning at his home in Pretoria, South Africa by a burglar. Pistorius shot through the locked door of the toilet a total of four times with his Taurus PT917 9mm pistol, killing his girlfriend, Reeva Steenkamp who was in the bathroom at the time and who Oscar Pistorius claimed he believed was an intruder... Using the toilet?

Pistorius was arrested for murder in 2013 and over a year later he was found guilty of culpable homicide (manslaughter) and jailed for five years. However, he was released from prison after only serving a year of his sentence. Then just two months after his release, the Supreme Court overturned his previous culpable homicide conviction, instead this time, finding him guilty of murder. Oscar Pistorius was eventually given a six-year sentence for the killing, though many people felt that the new sentence was still too lenient. In 2017, prosecutors successfully appealed to have his sentence lengthened to a total of thirteen years. And then in 2018, Oscar launched an appeal against his thirteen-year sentence, which he lost and is now currently serving his time in a South African prison for the murder of Reeva Steenkamp.

JOHN LANDIS

One of the most famous and popular film directors of the eighties. John Landis' big break came in 1978 with the raucous comedy hit, *Animal House*. He followed that up with one of the greatest musical films ever made, *The Blues Brothers* and even more classic films followed like *An American Werewolf in London* and *Trading Places* to name a few. But it was while filming the 1983 flick, *Twilight Zone: The Movie* when Death reared his head.

Twilight Zone: The Movie is a horror anthology film based on the cult TV show of the same name. The film featured multiple stories, each directed by a different person. John Landis' segment told the tale of a bigoted racist played by screen legend, Vic Morrow, who is sent to various time-periods and experiences what it would be like as one of the people he loved to ridicule. One particular scene saw Morrow's character in the midst of the Vietnam war being hunted by American soldiers. One part had his character attempt to rescue two Vietnamese children as a helicopter hovered overhead and Vic Morrow was meant to carry the two children under his arms as he ran underneath the copter through a body of water, all while controlled explosions and gunfire went off around him.

The story goes that it was an extremely dangerous stunt that involved a real helicopter. So dangerous was the stunt that both Vic Morrow and the pilot of the copter (who was a genuine Vietnam veteran) expressed concern over the lack of safety what with using a real helicopter and controlled explosions everywhere. Still, John Landis wanted his big shot for his film and ignored the concerns of his lead actor and skilled helicopter pilot. The cameras rolled and John shouted 'action', calling for the copter to hover closer and closer to the ground as Vic Morrow with a child tucked under each arm ran across a pool of water while flames, gunfire and pyrotechnic explosions added to the scene.

As Morrow ran under the helicopter, he accidentally dropped one of the children, 6-year-old Renee Shin-Yi Chen. At the same time, a mistimed explosion caught the tail-end of the low hovering helicopter, which caused it to crash to the ground. The landing skid of the copter crushed Renee Shin-Yi Chen to death as it fell. The helicopter then slumped onto its side which caused the rotor blades to come closer and closer to the ground. Vic Morrow and the second child, 7-year-old Myca Dinh Le were both decapitated by the fast-spinning blades. After the stunt, Vic Morrow was supposed to say the scripted line:

"I'll keep you safe, kids. I promise. Nothing will hurt you, I swear to God."

Sadly instead, all three of them died in the most horrific way. An inquest was held against both the production studio and John Landis himself that lasted several years. During the inquest, it was discovered that the children had been hired illegally, so shouldn't have even been on the set to begin with. But the deaths themselves were ruled as an unavoidable accident and John Landis was charged with involuntary manslaughter. However, in 1987, he was acquitted of the charges. The incident harmed John's carer for years during the trial, but after he was acquitted of the charges, he was back making films again. The families of the two children settled out of court, along with the family of Vic Morrow, one of which being his daughter and actress Jennifer Jason Leigh. In an interview about the accident, John Landis said:

"The special effects man who made the mistake by setting off a fireball at the wrong time was never charged."

Maybe so... But he didn't illegally hire two small children and have an already nervous and unprepared actor do the job of a trained stuntman, an actor who expressed his concern over the stunt, while the director kept calling for the helicopter to hover lower and lower did he Mr Landis?

PHIL SPECTOR

One of the most famous and influential songwriters & music producers ever. Phil Spector has written songs for and produced some of the biggest names in music history. The likes of Ben E. King, The Beatles, Gene Pitney, Righteous Brothers, Ike & Tina Turner to name a few have all had major worldwide hits thanks to Phil Spector. If you have a favourite song from the sixties or seventies, chances are that Spector had a hand in it somehow.

Phil Spector became semi-retired and withdrew from the public in the late sixties but made a comeback in the seventies when he worked with The Beatles on their *Get Back* album. Through the seventies, Spector became more and more reclusive, but he still worked with big-name artists now and again. By the eighties, Spector had pretty much fully retired only very, very occasionally working with music artists from that point onwards and was hardly heard about anymore, until 2003.

It was the 3rd of February, 2003 when actress and model, Lana Clarkson was found dead in Phil Spector's mansion in Alhambra, California. Clarkson had been shot and her body was found slumped in a chair with a single gunshot wound to her face, her blood and teeth were found scattered on the floor. Phil Spector later said how her death was an accidental suicide and that Lana Clarkson had actually tried to 'kiss the gun'. It was Spector's limo driver who raised the alarm when he reportedly said that he saw Phil Spector emerge from his mansion with a gun in his hand, and Spector supposedly said:

"I think I've killed someone."

Phil Spector's trial began on the 19th of March, 2007 which eventually led to a mistrial. So another trial began on the 20th of October, 2008 and that one took until the 13th of April, 2009 when the jury finally found Phil Spector guilty of murder in the second degree. Between then and now, several appeals have been launched, none of them have been successful. Phil Spector is currently serving a nineteen-years to-life prison term and will be eligible for parole in 2025 when he will be 88-years-old… If he's still alive of course. Edit: he dead now.

CHRISTIAN BRANDO

Christian Brando began his acting career as a child in 1968 when he was just 10 years old. Through the eighties and nineties, he also appeared in a handful of movies and TV productions using the alias Gary Brown as he didn't want to live in the shadow of his extremely famous father, you know the multi Oscar-winning actor (one he refused, the only person to ever refuse an Oscar), the Godfather himself, Marlon Brando.

Cheyenne Brando, the half-sister of Christian was in a relationship with Dag Drollet and was eight months pregnant with his child in 1990. On the 16th of May, 1990 Christian and Cheyenne went for dinner at the famed Musso & Frank Grill in Los Angeles. During dinner, Cheyenne Brando told her half brother that Dag had been physically abusive toward her on numerous occasions, even while she was pregnant. Upon returning to the Brando house, Christian confronted Dag about the alleged abuse when a fight broke out. During the fight, Christian pulled out a gun, which he claimed he only wanted to use to scare Dag. The gun went off and Dag was killed, as Christian recalled in an interview when he said:

"I just sat there and watched the life go out of this guy."

Dag, who was aged just 26 at the time of his death, possibly didn't even abuse Cheyenne Brando at all, as she claimed. It was later revealed that she suffered from mental health issues and this made Christian question whether his half-sister actually told him the truth or not. Christian Brando was put on trial for first-degree murder. However, as one of the main witnesses (Cheyenne Brando) had been admitted into a psychiatric hospital in Tahiti, and so couldn't testify, prosecutors couldn't prove that Dag's death was premeditated. This resulted in Christian being offered a plea bargain. His father Marlon, famously took the stand for a reduced sentence for his son during a televised court appearance where the Oscar-winning actor said:

"I think that perhaps I failed as a father. I'm certain that there were things that I could have done differently, had I known better at the time, but I didn't."

Christian pleaded guilty to the lesser charge of manslaughter and spent five years in prison. In 1995, before her brother was released, Cheyenne Brando committed suicide via hanging after losing custody of her son, she was just 25 years old. On the 26th of January, 2006, Christian Brando died of pneumonia at the Hollywood Presbyterian Medical Center. He was 49.

S. L. PERRIN

MICHAEL MASSEE

Popular character and small role actor, Michael Massee had a very distinctive face, one that was hard to forget. His name may not instantly jump out at you, but you'd definitely recognise him if you saw him. Appearing in films such as *Seven*, *Lost Highway*, *Amistad* and *The Amazing Spider-Man* to name a few, through the nineties and two-thousands in supporting roles. One of his earlier film roles was the dark, supernatural comic book flick *The Crow* starring Brandon Lee, son of legendary martial arts actor Bruce Lee.

During filming on the 31st of March, 1993, Brandon Lee was shot and killed in a tragic accident. The scene being filmed called for Brandon's character to return home to find his fiancée being attacked by street thugs. One of the thugs, played by Michael Massee, was to shoot Brandon with a Smith & Wesson Model 629 .44 Magnum revolver as he entered the room. An earlier shot of the film required a close up of the gun to be filmed to show that the weapon was loaded. Now, obliviously using live ammo for a film shoot is a big no-no! So dummy bullets were used with no powder or primer, so they looked just like the real thing but would not actually fire like real bullets.

When it came to filming the scene where the gun was to actually be fired, the dummy bullets were removed and replaced with blanks that sound and fire like real bullets, but as there is no actual bullet, nothing is actually fired from the gun. However, part of the previously used dummy bullet became trapped in the barrel of the gun. The gun was fired with the blanks, the force of the explosion worked just like a real bullet and shot the lodged dummy round out of the barrel, which then hit Brandon in the abdomen, mortally wounding him. At first, the cast and crew didn't realise that Brandon had been shot for real and believed he was just acting as he staggered backwards and slumped against the wall. But when a crew member noticed that real blood began to pool on the floor where Brandon was sitting, they soon realised that something had gone very wrong.

Brandon Lee was rushed to the New Hanover Regional Medical Center in Wilmington, North Carolina where he had to undergo six hours of surgery to try and save his life, but he sadly died aged 28-years-old at

1:03 PM on the 31st of March, 1993. And the person who pulled the trigger of the gun that killed him was Michael Massee. Over the years, Massee never really talked about that fateful day in 1993. Feeling deep guilt for killing Brandon Lee, even though it was not his fault at all, just a tragic accident, an accident that forced him to quit acting for a while. In fact, he only ever talked on camera once about how he felt about the incident in an interview with ExtraTV in 2005 (you can find it on YouTube) where Michael Massee talks about how he still has nightmares about the shooting. He said about the accidental shooting that claimed Brandon Lee's life how:

"I don't think you ever get over something like that."

Suffering from severe guilt, depression and nightmares over Lee's death for the rest of his life, Michael Massee died of cancer on the 20th of October, 2016.

ASININE DEATHS

Death can be heroic and meaningful, but sometimes it can be utterly trivial too. This chapter is all about people who have been killed for extremely asinine and pointless reasons by their killers. Murders and deaths, that just doesn't make any logical sense no matter how you try to rationalise them and go to show just how little human life can mean to some people.

THE SCHOOL SHOOTER

It was the 29th of January, 1979, a Monday. Brenda Spencer, 16 lived directly across the street from the Grover Cleveland Elementary School in San Diego, California. The children began lining up outside of the school that Monday morning, ready to start their school day and waited patiently for Principal Burton Wragg to open the gates as they did every school day as normal. Meanwhile, Spencer sat in her bedroom of her home, just watching the children line up outside of the school. She had previously been arrested for shooting the windows of the school with a BB gun. It was during Christmas, 1978 when her father decided to give Brenda a Ruger 10/22 semi-automatic .22 calibre rifle with a telescopic sight for a gift... A gift she would use for murder. Brenda Spencer sat in her house with that Christmas gift held tightly in hand and began shooting at the children.

Principal Burton Wragg was shot and killed trying to protect his pupils, along with school caretaker Mike Suchar. Also, eight children were injured, as was a police officer who had responded to the emergency call of the shooting. The shooting only stopped when the police managed to park a bin lorry in front of Brenda Spencer's house to obscure her line of sight. After firing thirty rounds, Spencer barricaded herself in her room and refused to come out. She spoke to a reporter from The San Diego Union-Tribune over the phone and when the reporter asked why Spencer started shooting at the school children, she infamously replied:

"I don't like Mondays. This livens up the day."

Perhaps you've heard The Boomtown Rats song, *I Don't Like Mondays* which is inspired by these events?

24

Several hours later, Brenda Spencer finally surrendered and left her house after being promised a Burger King meal from the police negotiator. She was charged with two counts of murder and assault with a deadly weapon ,of which she pleaded guilty to. Spencer was sentenced to twenty-five years to life on the 4th of April 1980, the day after her 18th birthday. Brenda Spencer has been refused her application for parole a total of five times so far. Her latest parole hearing was in August of 2019 and was refused yet again, so she still remains in prison today as of writing. So, just because Brenda Ann Spencer didn't like Mondays, two people were killed.

THE MATRIX DEFENCE

It had been a particularity cold and very snowy morning and on the 17th of February, 2003 in Fairfax, Virginia. 19-year-old Joshua Cooke had been helping his adoptive parents, Paul and Margaret, shovel snow from their driveway. After finishing his chore, Cooke went up to his room, looked at the poster for the film *The Matrix* he had on his wall and smiled. Cooke then got dressed up in combat boots and a trench coat, just like Keanu Reeves on the poster of the movie. He picked up a shotgun he had purchased just a few days earlier, loaded it and went back downstairs.

Joshua Cooke's father, Paul, was on the phone with Joshua's sister, Tiffany at the time of the shooting. Cooke shot his mother in the chest before turning his attention to his father when he fired a total of six more times. His father dived under a desk for cover, all while Joshua's sister helplessly heard the screams of her parents and the shooting over the phone. Cooke walked over to his wounded father, picked up the phone and spoke to his sister. Tiffany said to him:

"Josh, what are you doing? Let me talk to Daddy."

But he just hung up on her without saying a word and turned his attention back to his parents. Both Paul and Margaret were wounded, yet still amazingly alive. Joshua realised that he was out of ammo, so he calmly went back upstairs to his room and reloaded the shotgun before returning to the scene of his crime to finish what he had started. As he walked back down the stairs, his mother was clutching her chest in pain, as the blood dripped from her shotgun wound and asked:

"What are you doing Joshua? Why did you do this?"

His reply? He just pointed the newly loaded shotgun at her face and pulled the trigger. Joshua Cooke then stepped over the dead body of his mother and casually walked towards where his father was lying bleeding on the floor, behind the desk and shot him once in the head.

After the double murder, Joshua Cooke went back up to his room and opened a can of Coke before calling the police to inform them of what he had just done. The police soon arrived to find Cooke unarmed and remarkably calm, still drinking his Coke. They also discovered the bloody dead bodies of his parents lying on the floor.

Joshua Cooke originally pleaded not guilty by reason of insanity. He claimed that he was living in *The Matrix* movie, a virtual reality world that didn't really exist and so the murders didn't actually happen. This fast became known as '*The Matrix* defence', yes this defence has been used so many times over the years that it actually has its own name. However, during his trial for the double murder, Cooke changed his plea to guilty and confessed he was fully aware of what he did. During an interview for *Piers Morgan Live* on the CNN channel, Joshua Cooke said:

"I had no emotion at all. I was basically like a zombie. I just, I didn't care about anything anymore."

Joshua was sentenced to forty years in jail for murdering his adoptive parents who had been taking care of him since he was 5 years old, just because he watched *The Matrix* too many times and because he just didn't care anymore.

THE CONCERT TICKETS

Robert Lyons was a 39-year-old man who had been living in the same condo he shared with his mother, Linda Bolek in Carol Stream, Illinois. Lyons had moved in with his mother after he found himself in financial difficultly while living on his own. It was the 14th of March, 2008 when Robert Lyons asked his mother to buy him tickets to an Avril Lavigne concert which he really wanted to attend. His mother, Bolek, refused and an argument ensued. The pair began shouting at each other and Lyons lost his temper as he grew angrier and angrier with his mother. Grabbing a nearby bottle of cognac, he swung it at his mother's head hitting her, he swung again and struck her a second time, she fell to the floor of the kitchen. Linda Bolek was alive but unconscious. Robert Lyons then got hold of two kitchen knives and began stabbing his own unconscious mother in the back as she lay helpless on the floor. He stabbed her a total of nine times. So frantic was the attack that the blade of one of the knives broke off inside her body. He just stabbed, stabbed and stabbed until he was sure his mother was dead.

Even though his mother was most definitely dead, Lyons was not finished yet as next, he tried to destroy any DNA/forensic evidence. Using various under the sink household chemicals, including insecticide and drain cleaner, he poured them over the dead body of his mother before fleeing the scene. Police were eventually alerted by neighbours who'd overheard the argument, but by the time they arrived, Robert Lyons was long gone and Linda Bolek was dead on the floor lying in a pool of her own blood and household chemicals. A search for the killer ensued and Lyons was soon arrested, only a few hours later at a Hooters bar where the police had managed to track him down.

Robert Lyons' trial lasted only six days after which, the jury deliberated for no more than two hours before finding Lyons guilty of first-degree murder. He was sentenced to serve forty years in prison in September 2011. A mother gave life to her son and he took hers in return just because she refused to buy him tickets to an Avril Lavigne concert.

THE PHOTOBOMBING

It was during the early hours of the morning, a little after midnight of the 18th of January, 2014 in Santa Ana, California. Annie Hung Kim Pham was enjoying a night out with friends at The Crosby nightclub when she walked past a group of people taking a photo outside of the popular night-spot, a photo that Kim Pham accidentally walked into. What should've been resolved with a simple apology turned into something far more sinister and macabre.

There were two females from the group who were posing for the photo, Candace Brito and Vanesa Zavala. They both lashed out at Annie Hung Kim Pham and beat her mercilessly. Kicks and punches flew in a rage, as a brutal and bloody attack was carried out. Kim Pham fell to the ground unconscious, but the attack didn't stop there as her attackers, Brito and Zavala continued the beating while their victim lay on the floor bleeding. As the inhumane beating went on, people gathered around, some even filming the brutal thrashing on their phones with no one attempting to step in to stop it. Instead, several more joined in on the attack as a total of five people began kicking and stomping a bloodied and unconscious Annie Hung Kim Pham on the ground. The frenzied assault continued for several minutes until the attackers finally fled the scene. Annie Hung Kim Pham was rushed to the hospital where she was placed on life-support. Only two days later and she was declared brain dead and her life-support was turned off at the request of her family. Annie Hung Kim Pham was known as a very friendly and helpful person to those who knew her, always willing to lend a hand if needed. Her organs were later used to save the lives of others as she was an organ donor, so even after death, she was still helping those in need.

The two main attackers, Candace Brito and Vanesa Zavala were put on trial for the killing where they pleaded not guilty, claiming that they had acted in self-defence. They stated that it was Annie Hung Kim Pham who threw the first punch and they had every right to defend themselves. Though friends of Kim Pham refuted this claim, knowing of her kind and calm nature. Regardless of who started the fight, the jury found both Candace Brito and Vanesa Zavala guilty of manslaughter and assault. The two women were given a six-year prison sentence each and were ordered to pay for Annie Hung Kim Pham's funeral costs. At the sentencing the judge said:

"Why didn't you walk away? You're not gang members. You're not
fig'   You had been law-abiding, nice young women. And yet… You
          'he fight up to your elbows. If any of you had just swallowed
          and walked away, none of us would be sitting here."

                    'estigating coroner that the beating of Annie Hung
                     ' that it was simply impossible to tell which of

the many, many blows was the one that eventually killed her. The other three people who joined in on the attack were never found. Nobody won the fight that night with two young women in prison and another dead... Due to walking in the way of a photo being taken.

THE PARKING SPACE

Brian Stevenson was an off-duty detective working for the Baltimore Police Department protecting and serving the residents of Baltimore, Maryland for eighteen years. Stevenson was out with a friend for a few drinks and diner to celebrate his up and coming birthday on the night of Saturday the 16th of October, 2010. As Stevenson pulled into a parking space, 25-year-old Sian James approached the car just as Brian Stevenson exited his vehicle and instigated an argument with the detective over the parking space.

The men continued to argue as Brian Stevenson relied on his police training and did the best he could to try and de-escalate the situation. Believing he had succeeded in calming Sian James down, he began to walk away. This was when James picked up a hand-sized piece of concrete from the floor and hurled it toward the off-duty police officer. The projectile hit Stevenson in the head and knocked him to the floor. Brian Stevenson had suffered a massive head injury. Sian James quickly disappeared into the night and fled the scene. The police were called and worked fast by questioning witnesses who were at the busy night-spot at the time of the attack, and Sian James was soon arrested just a few hours later in a nightclub.

Brian Stevenson was rushed to the Johns Hopkins Bayview Medical Center where emergency crews did their best to save his life, but he was pronounced dead less than an hour before he was to due turn 38-years-old. Sian James was found guilty of first-degree murder and given a ten-year prison sentence. Brian Stevenson is survived by his wife and four children, who were left fatherless. Stevenson was a hard-working and thoroughly dedicated police officer, who would often put his life before others. A hard-working officer who, after serving on the force for nearly two decades, ended up losing his life over something as trivial as a parking simple spot.

S. L. PERRIN

THE SOCIAL MEDIA SPAT

Jenelle Potter moved to Mountain City, Tennessee, in 2005. She suffered from type-1 diabetes and was cared for by her parents, Barbara and Marvin Potter. Due to her illness, Jenelle would rarely leave the house and often used Facebook to make friends. Billie Jean Hayworth and her boyfriend Billy Payne were a local couple who had friended Jenelle on social media. After a while, the Facebook friendship began to sour and petty arguments between Jenelle Potter and Billie Jean Hayworth began to regularly appear online.

The inane feud continued for a while until Jenelle Potter unfriended Billy Payne after which, Billie Jean Hayworth then unfriended Jenelle in return. Then on the 31st of January, 2012, a friend of both Billie Jean Hayworth and Billy Payne visited their home and found the couple dead. Billy Payne was discovered in his bed with a single gunshot to his face, as well as having his throat slit. While Billie Jean Hayworth was also found dead with a single gunshot wound to her face. Bizarrely, she was also still cradling their 7-month-old baby boy who had survived the double murder, unharmed but the baby was splattered in his mother's blood and screaming when he was found. Due to the Facebook spat, Jenelle Potter became a major suspect for investigating police. After a while, it was her father, Marvin Potter who confessed to the double murder citing continual cyber-bullying of his daughter from Billie Jean Hayworth and Billy Payne as a reason for the double murder.

The police conducted a search of Jenelle's parent's house where she lived and even impounded Marvin's truck as evidence. In his truck were more than one-hundred printed pages that had been shredded into thousands and thousands of pieces, which the police meticulously reconstructed. The pages turned out to be hundreds of emails sent to the Potter family from a CIA agent called Chris. Chris had been sending the emails to Barbara and Marvin Potter warning them about threats on their daughter's life from both Billie Jean Hayworth and Billy Payne on Facebook. The investigating police also confiscated the computer used by the Potter family and after a thorough analysis, they soon learned that the emails from CIA agent Chris had actually been sent from same the IP address as the Potter's home. Meaning the emails were sent from their own house. Further investigation revealed that CIA agent Chris never existed at all and the emails were sent from Jenelle Potter to her parents herself to try and goad them into killing the perfectly innocent couple and it sadly worked too.

In October of 2013, Marvin Potter was found guilty of the murders and given two life sentences for the crime, one for each murder... But he didn't act alone. It took a further three years before both Jenelle Potter and her mother Barbara were put on trial for their involvement in and for the planning of the murders. The jury found both Jenelle and Barbara guilty of first-degree murder as well as being guilty of conspiracy to commit first-degree murder, and they were both sentenced to life in prison in July 2015. A 7-month-old baby made an orphan due to a petty argument over Facebook that never really happened.

THE LOUD MUSIC

17-year-old Jordan Davis was sitting in the SUV owned by his friend Tommie Stornes, along with two other friends, Leland Brunson and Tevin Thompson. They had parked in a gas station in Jacksonville, Florida on the 23rd of November, 2012. Stornes had gone into the gas station but left the SUV running so his friends could listen to some music while they waited. It was around 7:30 PM when Michael David Dunn pulled into the same gas station next to the SUV where the three youths were listening to music while waiting for their friend to return. Dunn was accompanied by his girlfriend Rhonda Rouer who exited the car and headed for the gas station to buy some supplies for the hotel room they were staying in. The loud rap music coming from the SUV began to annoy Michael Dunn who asked for it to be turned down. At first one of the teenagers, Tevin Thompson did turn the music down but Jordan Davis quickly turned it back up. The two parties remained in their respective vehicles as an argument between Michael Dunn and the teenagers kicked off and began to escalate.

Eventually, Michael Dunn pulled out a handgun from his glove box and fired at the SUV, hitting the door of the seat where Jordan Davis was sitting. The bullets tore through the car door and into Davis, hitting him in the legs, lungs, and aorta. The driver, Tommie Stornes had returned at this point and managed to get the SUV into reverse to try and get away from the gunfire. This was when Dunn got out of his car and continued shooting at the petrified teens. Stornes started driving the SUV away from the carnage unaware that one of his friends had been shot multiple times. He eventually pulled into a car park when finally away from the danger and noticed that Jordan Davis was struggling to breathe and gasping for air.

It was the next morning while watching TV in their hotel room when Michael Dunn's girlfriend, Rhonda Rouer, watched a news report revealing that 17-year-old Jordan Davis had been shot and killed. The pair drove back to their home at Satellite Beach, Florida without reporting the crime, thankfully an eyewitness contacted the police and reported Dunn's license plate number and he was arrested at his home the following day.

Michael Dunn stood trial on the 15th of February, 2014 and after more than thirty hours of deliberation, he was found guilty of three counts of attempted second-degree murder for shooting at Tommie Stornes, Leland Brunson and Tevin Thompson. But the jury could not reach an agreement on the charge of first-degree murder of Jordan Davis, so the judge called for a mistrial. Dunn's retrial started on the 22nd of September, 2014 and he was eventually found guilty of the murder of Jordan Davis on the 1st of October. Michael Dunn was sentenced to life in prison without parole for the first-degree murder of Jordan Davis as well as three consecutive thirty-year sentences for the attempted second-degree murder of the teenager's friends, who were in the car with him, and an additional fifteen years for shooting into a moving vehicle.

In January 2015, a documentary film covering the shooting and the following trial titled: *3 1/2 Minutes, 10 Bullets* was released. The film was nominated for and even won several awards. Four teenagers shot at with one dying from his wounds just because someone didn't like their loud music.

THE BABYSITTER TEXT

Husband and wife, Chad and Nicole Oulson decided to take in a movie on the 13th of January, 2014 in Tampa, Florida. Their film of choice was the tense drama *Lone Survivor*. Along with several other people attending the movie were another married couple, Curtis and Vivian Reeves. Curtis Reeves was a retired, 71-year-old police captain. The Reeves sat directly behind the Oulsons and waited for the film to begin. It was that time before the lights dimmed and the adverts and trailers began, while people found a seat ready to enjoy the movie. So the film had not yet started proper.

Chad Oulson decided to take the time before the start of the movie to check in on the babysitter looking after their daughter back at their home. He took out his phone and send a quick text, that was when Curtis Reeves leaned forward and complained to Chad about using his phone during the movie despite the fact it hadn't even started yet. A heated exchange of words began between the two men. Curtis Reeves then said he was going to get the manager and promptly left the theatre in search of someone to complain to. By now, the lights had dimmed as the previews and ads begun, yet this was still before the film had begun. After a while, Curtis Reeves returned and witnesses claim he was clearly agitated, he sat back down in his seat where the argument between the two men continued.

It's reported that Chad Oulson threw some popcorn at Curtis Reeves and this was when Curtis pulled out a handgun from his pocket and fired a single shot. At the same time Nicole Oulson raised her hand to her husband's chest to try to calm him down, Nicole was hit in the hand and suffered a minor gunshot wound to her finger. Her husband was not so lucky. The same bullet hit Chad in the chest killing him. Police were called and Curtis Reeves was arrested at the scene.

During the initial trial, Curtis Reeves used Florida's controversial 'stand your ground defence'. A defence, that establishes a right by which a person may defend one's self or others against threats or perceived threats, even to the point of applying lethal force. So Curtis Reeves claimed that his life was in danger from the thrown popcorn and he had every right to defend himself. In 2017, the judge eventually ruled that Curtis was not acting in self-defence when he fired the gun at Chad Oulson as thrown popcorn was not deemed a threat to life. Curtis Reeves has been ordered to wear an ankle monitor that restricts his movements while awaiting his next trial. As of writing, the trial against Curtis

Reeves for the second-degree murder of 43-year-old Chad Oulson continues and it's been over five years since that fateful day the Oulsons decided to go to the cinema. No matter the outcome, killing a man for throwing popcorn and using a phone in a cinema before the film has even started is deplorable. A young girl no longer has a father because of Curtis Reeves, a retired police captain's lack of self-control.

THE CHEETOS INCIDENT

It was a normal Tuesday night in downtown St. Louis, Missouri in September 2012. Two men, 49-year-old David Lynn Scott and 42-year-old Roger Wilkes were walking along the street when an argument between the two broke out. The argument escalated and grew worse until Scott pulled out a knife and plunged the sharp blade into the chest of Wilkes. A patrol officer saw the incident and called it in, also asking for an ambulance to help the stab victim. David Lynn Scott attempted to flee the scene while Roger Wilkes was rushed to a nearby hospital.

The officer on a police patrol bike gave chase and managed to catch David Lynn Scott, quickly arresting him. The knife he used for the stabbing was also recovered. His victim, Roger Wilkes later died from his injury while in hospital. But why did the initial argument that led to the murder begin? Well, Roger Wilkes had himself a nice big bag of the cheese puff snack, Cheetos and David Lynn Scott wanted some. But when Wilkes refused to share, Lynn became upset and then decided to pull out a knife and stab his victim once in the chest killing him. David Lynn Scott pleaded guilty to the second-degree murder charge and was ordered to serve twenty-three years in prison… Over some Cheetos.

THE WORLD CUP MATCH

David Makoeya was a 61-year-old husband and father from a small village in Limpopo, South Africa. He was a keen football fan and wanted to watch the opening World Cup game between Germany and Australia on the 13th of June, 2010. However, his wife and two adult children didn't, they wanted to watch a local religious programme. His 68-year-old wife, Francina changed the channel to the religious show via the remote control. Then, when David got up to change the channel back to the football by hand, he was brutally attacked by his own family.

BOOK OF DEATHS

David's wife Francina was joined by their 36-year-old son, Colin and 23-year-old daughter, Lebogang. The family later claimed they were not exactly sure what happened, that they couldn't even remember what they initially used to begin the attack. However, they did recall smashing David's head against a wall and that was when he fell to the floor motionless. The family quickly called the police after it became clear that the husband and father was seriously injured, but by the time the emergency services arrived, he was dead.

The wife and two children were arrested at the scene. The daughter was released on bail while the mother and son remained in custody until their day in court. I couldn't actually find what sentence (if any) the mother and children were given for the killing of their own family member. But regardless, a husband and father is dead due to an argument over wanting to watch a football game and control of the TV.

THE LACK OF A THANKS

Wainuiomata, New Zealand is where unemployed, 36-year-old Fergus John Glen lived, in the same house as his parents. His brother Craig had been having a bit of a rough time with his personal life after he had recently split from his wife. So in an act of brotherly love, Fergus invited his down on his lick brother round for a nice meal, a few drinks and to stay the night on the 7th of March, 2003. A nice slice of family bonding with Fergus hoping he could cheer his brother up a bit. Everyone had a great time and all went to bed later that night, everyone except Fergus. He decided to stay up a little while and drink some whiskey… Lots of whiskey. There had always been a few arguments between the brothers over the years, but all brothers disagree at one time or another. You move on, forgive and forget, something Fergus just could not do.

After drinking his whiskey, Fergus calmly then walked down to the basement and picked up the axe the family often used to chop firewood. He then walked upstairs to where the bedrooms were and where his brother was fast asleep. According to the police, the mother was woken by what she described as:

"wood-chopping noises."

35

Those noises were her son, Craig being murdered by her other son. Fergus brought the axe down on his sleeping brother a total of eight times across the neck and face. One of the many wounds that Craig suffered via the axe was one that severed his spine.

As Fergus returned the axe to the basement, he met his mother on the stairs who was woken by the noises and he simply said:

> "I've done him with an axe."

But why this horrific act of fratricide anyway? Well, Fergus told police that he decided to kill his own brother because Craig hadn't thanked him for the meal he provided that night. As Fergus told police at the time:

> "He just annoyed me and I did it."

Fergus John Glen was arrested and sentenced to life in prison for the brutal and bloody axe murder of his own brother. He became eligible for parole after serving ten years in March 2013. But the parole board declined to release Fergus believing that he was still an undue risk to the safety of the community. One brother kills the other because of a lack of a thanks for dinner.

THE NO TOILET PAPER MURDER

56-year-old Franklin Paul Crow and 58-year-old Kenneth Matthews lived in the small town of Moss Bluff, Florida where they were room-mates. Matthews was a Vietnam War veteran who had a penchant for fishing, hunting and riding his motorbike. It was at Ma Barkers Hideaway, a local bikers bar where the pair first met. They began drinking and chatting and would regularly meet up at the bar. The pair soon learned that they had a lot in common and fast became friends over time and many more beers. After a while, Kenneth Williams asked Franklin Paul Crow to move into his apartment with him to help out with paying the bills and so on.

As friends and room-mates, they would occasionally argue and disagree, but on the whole, they got on well together. However, one disagreement would end in murder. The argument began when Kenneth Matthews noticed that the toilet paper had been used up, leaving only an empty cardboard tube. The two began to argue over the lack of toilet paper and eventually, Matthews grabbed his hunting rifle and threatened to kill his room-mate. This was when Crow picked up a sledgehammer handle and began to mercilessly beat his room-mate with it, hitting him eight times. Mathews fell to the floor of the apartment they shared but Crow was not done yet, he then got hold of a claw hammer and swung it at his so-called friend twice with the clawed end. The beating that Kenneth Matthews endured was so severe that he suffered a fractured skull, broken fingers and fatal wounds to his head. He was beaten so badly that he could not be recognised and was eventually formally identified by his fingerprints. Franklin Paul Crow fled the scene and Kenneth Matthews' body was discovered later by their landlord.

Crow was later tracked down by police and arrested for the murder. When questioned by police, he originally denied having anything to do with the killing but eventually confessed. He stood trial where Franklin Paul Crow pleaded guilty and was sentenced to serve twenty-two years in prison. While in prison he wrote to the judge that oversaw his trial and said:

"I have accepted the fact I'll never see my people again, or go fishing, or ride my motorcycle anymore. It is hard for me to stand down, but if I am in the wrong which I know I am, I am ready to except and deal with the circumstances."

A twenty-two-year prison sentence due to an argument over toilet paper.

THE FART

School kids can be very cruel, they can also turn to murder. Warrensville Heights, Ohio and 16-year-old Shaakira Dorsey was hanging out with a few other teenage friends after school. One of the group, and unnamed teen, also 16 let out a fart. This was when Dorsey began making jokes and teasing the teen over her passing gas, as the other school kids laughed. An argument kicked off as Shaakira Dorsey and the unnamed teen started to row. Suddenly, the nameless teen lashed out and struck Dorsey and a violent fight soon erupted between the two teens. The gathered school kids did nothing to stop the fight either.

Eyewitnesses say that Shaakira Dorsey was knocked to the ground, they also stated that they saw the attacking teen straddle Dorsey as she lay on the floor and began repeatedly punching her in the face over and over. The small gathered crowd began to grow and just watched the brutal beating, including adults. One of the adults was Shaakira Dorsey's own stepfather, who eventually broke the fight up by separating the fighting teens. As things began to calm down, Dorsey got herself up from the floor and began to pace back and forth, uneasy on her feet, disorientated and finding it difficult to breathe. She then just collapsed and fell face-first onto the grass outside the apartment complex where the fight began.

An ambulance rushed to the scene and took Shaakira Dorsey to the Ahuja Medical Center where she later died. Dorsey's unnamed attacker was tried at a juvenile court where she was found guilty of the murder. One 16-year-old dead and another serving time for murder over a little flatulence.

THE COLD BREAKFAST

It was a perfectly normal September morning, 2010 in Breathitt County, Kentucky. 47-year-old Stanley Neace woke up feeling hungry and ready for breakfast, in the mobile home he shared with his 54-year-old wife Sandra Neace. Also living in the mobile home was 28-year-old Sandra Strong, the daughter of Stanley's wife from a previous relationship and her boyfriend, 31-year-old Dennis Turner. They had parked their mobile home in a trailer park shared with several others. It was when Sandra Neace served her husband and family breakfast when the unbelievable horrors of that day began.

Stanley was not happy with his food and complained that his eggs were cold. An enraged Stanley got up from the breakfast table and retrieved his 12-gauge pump-action shotgun from the bedroom before returning to the table and began shooting. His step-daughter Sandra Strong and her boyfriend, Dennis Turner were both shot and killed at the breakfast table. His wife made a run for it in an attempt to find help. Eyewitnesses say they saw Stanley chase his wife around a car while shooting at her. Sandra Neace began crying and screaming for help, begging for her life but her cries were soon ended by her husband's shotgun.

More and more of the trailer park residents witnessed what was going on, so after murdering his wife, Stanley Neace turned his attention to them, firing at some of his neighbours, thankfully he missed. That was until 40-year-old Tammy Kilborn got involved, Kilborn came out of her home to see what all the commotion was about, Neace raised his shotgun and killed her as she stood in the entrance of her trailer. Stanley Neace then walked into the mobile home of 30-year-old Teresa Fugate and also murdered her as his rampage continued. Neace then turned his gun on the 7-year-old daughter of Fugate who had just witnessed her mother being brutally murdered. The 7-yearold reportedly said:

"Please, please don't shoot me."

Stanley paused for a few seconds before replying:

"All right, you can leave."

The terrified child ran away and that was when the police were finally alerted to the massacre by one of the neighbours. Stanley Neace then returned to his mobile home and witnesses claim he began talking and mumbling to himself while pacing up and down outside the door of his mobile home. The police eventually arrived, and that was when Neace turned the gun on himself and fired one final shot. A total of six people died that day, Stanley Neace's five victims and Neace himself via suicide, because he felt his eggs for breakfast were not hot enough.

THE NON-BELIEVER

Back in February of 2012, human remains were discovered, buried in a shallow grave in Clay County, Texas. The body was face down in the grave and covered by numerous bits of debris. It was later revealed that the remains belonged to SPC. Jose Ramirez, a junior army enlistee who mysteriously went missing several years previously. A former friend of the deceased was soon found guilty of the murder, 30-year-old Justin Green. After an investigation, it was eventually discovered that Ramirez was shot and killed by Green sometime in 2007, in the bedroom of a residence close to where the body was found in its shallow grave. But it turns out that Justin Green did not act alone. After the murder, he called up both his mother and sister and they turned up to clean up the crime scene by removing the blood, they then even helped to move the body to its final resting place. Then after burying the body, the trio used Jose Ramirez's credit card to order pizza, drinks and sat around enjoying the food the victim had just paid for.

But just why was Jose Ramirez killed? Well, because he was an atheist. Justin Green was a devout Christian and an argument between the two men about religion got out of hand. While being questioned by police over the murder, Green's sister stated that Ramirez was killed because he didn't believe in God. Justin Green shot Jose Ramirez twice due to his lack of faith in a higher power. Green was found guilty of first-degree murder and he was sentenced to serve thirty years in prison. So much for the 5th commandment eh, whatever happened to thou shalt not kill?

THE SLOW SANDWICH

Noisy-le-Grand is a small commune in Paris, France and home to several small local businesses. On the 16th of August, 2019 a small fast food restaurant called Mistral would be the site of a pointless argument that would lead to cold-blooded murder.

A customer ordered a sandwich from the restaurant and patiently waited for his food to be made. However, the customer's patience began to run thin after waiting several minutes for his order. The angry customer began to argue with the staff, feeling his order was taking way too long. A 28-year-old waiter stepped forward in an attempt to calm down the irate customer. Witnesses claim that during the argument, the customer began shouting at and insulting the waiter before producing a 9-millimetre handgun and shooting the restaurant employee at around 9:15 PM. Other staff called the emergency services, but the waiter died of his injuries shortly after paramedics arrived and was pronounced dead at the scene. The gunman fled the scene and as of writing, is still being hunted by local police for killing a restaurant worker just because he felt his sandwich was not being made fast enough.

THEME PARK DEATHS

I'm a big fan of theme parks and have many happy memories visiting them too. The excitement of the rides, the smell of the food all plays a big part in the enjoyment. But now and then, things do not go according to plan and these happy, exciting places can also be places of death via accidents, stupidity, suicide and even murder.

HAUNTED CASTLE

The Six Flags Great Adventure theme park in Jackson Township, New Jersey featured many popular rides and attractions. One of its most popular attractions was called the Haunted Castle, a dark and scary experience where visitors walk through various rooms featuring classic spooky iconography. Skeletons, ghouls, vampires and the like were represented via carefully dressed mannequins that would pop out from walls and around dark corners. Some of these monstrous characters were even played by made-up park employees to add an extra layer of realism.

The attraction also featured things like strobe lighting and other effects that would disorientate the visitors as they walked through the dark maze-like horror-themed castle. Under all that decoration was nothing short of a death trap as many of the materials used for the attraction's construction included plywood, foam rubber, tar paper as well as various plastics and fabrics, all highly flammable. So when a fire broke out on the 11th of May, 1984, the popular haunted house became an uncontrollable blaze within minutes.

At the time the fire broke out, Haunted Castle had around twenty-nine guests and employees trapped inside. Only fourteen of them managed to escape unscathed while seven others, who eventually got out, were treated for smoke inhalation. However, the final eight people were not so lucky. A small group of teens were trapped inside the blaze and died. Yet all while the fire was raging, the park remained open and continued to welcome guests as if nothing was wrong. Perhaps the most macabre twist is the fact that nobody knew that anyone was actually trapped inside and had died in the fire at first. They believed everyone got out safely but when the fire was finally under control and eventually extinguished by local fire-fighters and when they got inside the attraction, that was when the pile of eight badly burnt bodies were discovered and even then, they were initially mistaken for some of the mannequins used as décor to scare the patrons.

It wasn't until later that night when some of the teenagers failed to return home that the alarm was raised, then the connection between the missing youths and the charred remains inside the attraction was when the penny dropped. Emergency services soon learned those mannequins were in fact the charred bodies of school children. So badly burnt were the teenagers that they couldn't even be formally identified until much later, and even then only via dental records. Even to this day, it's never been established exactly how the fire started. There was a witness who claimed that he saw a teenager use a cigarette lighter to help illuminate the dark corridors and that the lighter set fire to some of the foam rubber used on the walls. But no one else saw this happen, so some believed the witness and the fire starter were one and the same, and that they came up with the story to detract from their guilt. But when the witness was cross-examined, he was ruled out as a suspect. To this day, no one has been held accountable for the deaths of the eight teenagers who died in the fire and the fire itself was officially ruled as being an accident.

An independent documentary film called *Doorway to Hell? The Mystery and Controversy Surrounding the Fire at the Haunted Castle*, which was released in 2002 explores the tragedy and questions the final ruling of the fire being an accident.

MINDBENDER COASTER

Found at Galaxyland Amusement Park in West Edmonton Mall, Alberta, Canada. The Mindbender roller coaster is famous for being the largest indoor triple-looping roller coaster in the world. Topping an impressive hight of one hundred and forty-five-foot and boasting a hundred and twenty-seven-foot drop, while able to reach a top speed of sixty miles per hour. The Mindbender is one of the most popular roller coasters in the world and certainty the most popular in Canada. But on the 14th of June, 1986, just one day after a safety inspector declared the ride to be safe was when tragedy struck.

The ride was operating as normal and had already entertained numerous thrill-seekers. But later that day, as the train of the coaster was full of passengers and as it reached its top speed of sixty miles per hour ready to rush through the third and final loop, the back of the train began to uncontrollably shake and rumble. The last car of the train derailed as it entered the loop of the ride and the safety lap bars disengaged which sent the four passengers of the car flying, they fell around twenty-five foot, smashing into the hard concrete ground. As the train lost momentum due to the derailment, it failed to make it through the loop and began to roll backwards. As the train rolled back along the track, back down the loop, it fishtailed wildly while gaining more and more speed and smashed into a concrete post wedging the train on the tracks. Three of the passengers who were thrown from the car, Tony Mandrusiak, Cindy Simms and David Sager died while the fourth, Rod Chayko was critically injured but survived. Another nineteen others were also treated for minor injures.

An investigation to the accident revealed that the bolt that held the wheels of the last car of the train on the track became loose. The bolts eventually snapped under the strain and this is what caused the wheels of the last car to come off. The train continued the pull the last car around due to the high speeds. At the same time, the now wheel-less car's undercarriage was sheared off, this is what caused the safety lap bars to disengage and throw its passengers from the car. Even now, no one has ever claimed responsibility for the accident and the direct cause has been ruled as undetermined. Though most people seem to believe a lack of maintenance was the main cause, despite the fact the coaster was checked and given the all-clear the day before the accident. Either way, three people are dead due to whatever the direct cause of the derailment actually was.

ACTION PARK DEATHS

Located in Vernon, New Jersey and opened in 1978. Action Park has become infamous among theme park fans for its many deaths and numerous injuries involving the park's rides and attractions over the years. So frequent the accidents and deaths have been at Action Park since it's opening, it has been given nicknames such as 'Traction Park' and 'Accident Park'. There have been so many deaths connected to the park that I decided to include them all in one sub-chapter.

The first death occurred in 1980 on an attraction called Alpine Slide, which was described by one patron of the park as:

"A giant track to rip people's skin off that was disguised as a kid's ride."

Basically, Alpine Slide was a long and twisting slide built from cement and fibreglass. You would be given a plastic toboggan on wheels which you would sit in to go down the slide. These toboggans would have breaks... Some of them worked and some didn't. A 19-year-old park employee was trying out the ride and speeding down the slide when his toboggan and he, flew off the track at one of the corners and he hit his head on a rock. He died eight days later from his injuries.

Tidal Wave Pool was a one hundred foot wide by two hundred and fifty-foot long swimming pool, that would generate huge waves every twenty minutes with ten-minute respites separating the waves. Some of the waves could easily reach a height of one meter and with several of them hitting you one after another, the pool soon earned it's very own nickname, 'The Grave Pool'. Around twelve lifeguards were always on duty at any one time during busy days and they would often have to save around thirty people a day. In 1982, 84 and 87, several people would not be so lucky as to be saved by the lifeguards as a 15-year-old boy, a 20-year-old man and an 18-year-old all drowned in the pool over those respective years.

The Kayak Experience was an attraction at Action Park that did exactly what it promised. Guests would climb into a kayak and then be sent down a white-water rapids styled experience. A lot of time, the kayaks would get stuck or tip over, leaving the guests to remedy the situation themselves. In 1982, a 27-year-old man found himself in that particular situation where his kayak had tipped over, so he tried to get it the right way up to continue the experience. However, as he attempted to correct his vessel, he came in contact with some live wiring under the water which was used to power fans that would agitate the water and create small waves on the surface. He suffered a severe electric shock, which sent him into cardiac arrest and was rushed to a nearby hospital but died soon after from a shock-induced cardiac arrest. Who'd've thought that electricity and water wasn't a good mix?

The Tarzan Swing was perhaps one of the simplest attractions at any theme park ever. You remember making rope swings as a kid? Well, that's pretty much what The Tarzan Swing was. A simple, but very large rope swing where guests would swing out and then let go, to drop into a large pool of water. The main issue was that the pool was filled with natural spring water, which would be far, far colder, at around 10°C, than the water used at other attractions around the park, which was 27°C. So many of the guests were not expecting just how cold the pool really was. In 1984 a visitor to the park decided to have a go at the swing and when he splashed into the pool, he suffered a fatal heart attack, which was triggered by the shock of the much colder water.

You know those tower drop kind of rides you find in every theme park everywhere, those ones you sit in and get carried up into the air and dropped back down again? Well, Action park had one of those too called Space Shot, it was one of the final rides ever built for the park. In 1994 Space Shot was undergoing testing before it would be opened to the public and one of those tests involved weight variances. A 22-year-old employee was sent up the one hundred and sixty-five-foot shaft of the tower in a carriage designed to take the park guests to the top of the tower at speed before dropping them down again. Several tests had already been successfully carried out that day but one more test would prove fatal. The carriage holding the 22-year-old employee was sent up the tower unsecured at the low speed of three miles per hour, but a malfunction suddenly caused the speed to increase to ten miles per hour and the 22-year-old lost his balance and plummeted around one-hundred and twenty-foot to the ground below killing him instantly.

A total of seven people have lost their lives at Action Park between the years of 1980 and 1994. Several lawsuits from the numerous injuries and deaths at the park eventually caused the place to close in 1996. Years later, the land was sold and the park reopened in 2014 as Action Park once more, before it was given a name change to Mountain Creek Waterpark from 2016 and is still in operation today and thankfully, no more deaths... Yet.

S. L. PERRIN

THE BIG DIPPER

The Big Dipper at Battersea Park in London opened at the Battersea Park Funfair, it was one of the biggest and most popular attractions in the whole of the UK at the time. Originally opened as part of the Festival of Britain in the summer of 1951. The Big Dipper was one of those early, wooden coasters made long before the invention of the modern steel monsters built these days. In 1970, a fire damaged the ride... But that's not what this one is about. As, after some repairs, The Big Dipper was reopened. On the 30th of May, 1972 is when disaster struck this hugely popular ride.

Battersea Park Funfair was bustling with parents and children, all excited to try out the recently restored The Big Dipper, after seeing it featured in the news on TV. The line began to grow for the ride and the trains were crammed full of happy passengers ready to be thrilled and scared at the same time by the speed and inclines of the ride. As the jam-packed train left the station and made its way up the incline for it's first of many drops, the rope that was used to haul the passenger loaded train up the hill snapped. The train, it's cars and all the riders began to roll backwards gathering more and more speed, heading back to the station full of people all lining up for the ride. The roll-back break also failed and despite his best efforts, the brake-man used to slow the ride in case of an emergency just could not reduce its ever-increasing speed.

The screams of the people on the ride were drowned out by the deafening noise of the train clanging down the track. As it made it to the base of the incline, the car at the back of the train came off the tracks when it hit a sharp turn at the bottom of the hill, and smashed through a barrier. The other two cars of the train crashed into the carnage. A total of thirteen people were seriously injured and five young children lost their lives.

One of the survivors, Carolyn Adamczyk who was only 14 at the time that fateful day in May of 1972, remembered her experience in an interview with The Independent newspaper in 2015:

"As soon as we started shooting backwards everything went into slow motion, I turned around and saw the brake-man desperately trying to put the brake on but it wasn't working. Most of the carriages didn't go around the bend, one detached and went off the side through a wooden hoarding. People were groaning and hanging over the edge. It was awful."

Carolyn Adamczyk soon found herself stuck in one of the cars of the train with a young and very scared little girl sitting next to her. They began to try and escape by walking along the tracks of the ride as Adamczyk remembers:

"This girl screamed that she wanted to get off, but she leant on a wooden barrier and it collapsed. I tried to grab for her, but I saw her fall to the ground in front of me. I told everyone to stay where they were as I tried to find a way down, but I realised as I was walking down that I was walking on blood. I looked up, and next to the carriage people were hanging out over the tracks. There was blood everywhere."

After the accident, The Big Dipper was closed and dismantled. The funfair's visitor numbers plummeted and the Battersea Park Funfair eventually closed in 1974.

SPACE JOURNEY

Ecoventure Valley is a popular theme park in Shenzhen, China. One of its rides, Space Journey was a space shuttle launch simulator, a bit like Mission: Space that is found in Epcot at Disney World. A centrifugal motion simulator that spins at high speed to recreate the kind of g-forces astronauts would experience. Space Journey had a capacity of forty-eight passengers, at the ride was at full capacity on the 29h of June 2010 when disaster struck.

As the ride was spinning at full speed, one of the carriages that housed its passengers broke away from the holding arm. The momentum of the ride meant the carriage began bouncing around and slamming into the other cabins and walls of the ride, while also falling around twelve meters to the ground. Witnesses said that that they first heard one loud bang followed by several others as the carriage broke free and began smashing into the others, followed by screams of terror as well as a strong smell of burning rubber.

Many of the riders were knocked unconscious and were not aware of what had happened until they were informed of the accident after they woke up in a hospital later, as one survivor recalls:

"There was a sudden loud boom inside the cabin. Then everything went black and I don't know what happened. I was in the hospital when I woke up."

Fire-fighters had to be called in to help free those trapped inside. Amazingly, some people managed to escape without injury however, ten other people were not so lucky and they sustained numerous injuries including broken bones, lacerations and bruises. All of the injured were rushed to the Shenzhen People's and Shenzhen Meisha Hospitals for immediate treatment.

Other than those injured, sadly, six other people lost their lives that day when two men and four women aged between 24 and 48 were killed. The Space Journey tragedy was the worst theme park accident ever in China. Another survivor recalls the incident:

"All the cabins but the one we were sitting in were destroyed. Some people fell onto the rail and some fell on the ground. Some people died instantly and were just hanging dead in their seats."

The disaster was ruled as a mechanical problem, but authorities never publicly revealed the specific problem that led to the six deaths.

THUNDER RIVER RAPIDS

The whole of the theme park, Dreamworld in Queensland, Australia had to be closed down for forty-five days after a catastrophe caused the death of four people. It was the 25th of October, 2016 when Cindy Low, 42, Kate Goodchild, 32, Luke Dorsett, 35 and Roozi Araghi, 38 were cooling down from the hot sun on the Thunder River Rapids ride. It was one of those popular attractions that can be found everywhere around the world, where riders sit in circular rafts and are propelled through a man-made series of rough waters through a pre-made track. Always under strict control even when it often feels like it isn't. The four adults killed also had two children with them in one of the boats on the ride.

BOOK OF DEATHS

Before the ride fully ends, the rafts are pulled up to the station area where passengers would disembark, this would always be the highest point on the ride and to get the rafts up to the station, a large conveyor belt would be used as the rafts would exit the water, to be pulled up to the station via the conveyor belt. It was at this point at the very end of the ride where disaster would strike.

Two water pumps used to keep the flow and level of the water consistent failed. The water level dropped and one of the rafts became stranded on some steel railings near the base of the conveyor belt. This was when the raft carrying the four victims bumped into the stranded one and flipped over. The two children were mercifully thrown clear and survived the incident, but the adults were not so lucky. All four victims were pulled toward the mechanism that powered the conveyor belt and the ever-flowing water made the situation even worse.

All four were dragged under the water and under the conveyor belt where they were crushed to death by the workings. The two children who were thrown clear of the disaster were the son of Cindy Low and the daughter of Kate Goodchild. So two small children witnessed their own mothers killed before their very eyes. The ride was stopped and the water drained so the bodies could be recovered. More than seven paramedic crews attended the recovery which lasted until the early hours of the following morning. So badly crushed by the conveyor belt workings were the bodies, that several of the paramedics who had to recover them required counselling due to the trauma of what they had witnessed. Thunder River Rapids was immediately closed down never to reopen and eventually dismantled.

HYDRO

16-year-old Hayley Williams was enjoying a family holiday in Pembrokeshire, Wales when the family decided to pay a visit to Oakwood Theme Park looking for some fun and excitement. Hydro was Europe's biggest, fastest and wettest water ride in 2004 and Haley wanted to try it out, sadly it would be the final theme park ride she would ever experience. Hydro was part steel roller coaster and part water ride. It takes it's passengers up to a hight of over one-hundred and twenty-feet, before rolling toward and over a steep, almost vertical plunge into a body of water at the base reaching speeds of fifty miles per hour, which creates a forty-five-foot wave as the boat carrying guests splashes down and through the water at the bottom of the drop.

Hayley got on the ride, while her family decided to sit it out and wait for her to return. It was while the boat carrying it's riders made its climb toward its summit when Hayley fell around a hundred-foot from the car she was in, hitting the steel structure of the ride, before landing in the water below. Hayley was rushed to hospital by air ambulance only for her to die of her injuries later. An inquest into the accident was carried out and closely analysed CCTV footage of the ride revealed that the lap restraint designed to hold the riders safely in place had not been checked by the staff. It was the loose restraint that led to Hayley falling to her death.

Oakwood Theme Park pleaded guilty to breaching the Health and Safety Act of 1974 and were ordered to pay a £250,000 fine as well as £80,000 in legal costs. Hydro was closed down for the investigation, but it reopened and was renamed Drench in 2011.

VERRÜCKT

Schlitterbahn Kansas City Waterpark in Kansas City, Kansas is home to some of the world's biggest and wildest water rides and slides. It opened in the summer of 2009 but on the 7th of August, 2016, a horrific incident would occur that would close down one of it's biggest and most popular attractions.

Verrückt, German for crazy or insane, was a one-hundred and sixty-eight-foot, seventy miles per hour water slide. Riders would have to climb a whopping two-hundred and sixty-four steps to reach the top. There, they would sit on small, three-person rafts to then speed down a seventeen storey plunge, before having to climb a five-storey incline to slow the riders down before it's second and final drop into a run-off pool. Verrückt was a fast and frantic water-slide. During its time, several minor injures caused by the speed and ferociousness of the ride were reported, but nothing serious ever happened... Until that fateful day in August 2016.

BOOK OF DEATHS

10-year-old Caleb Schwab wanted to experience the high-speed thrills of Verrückt for himself. He climbed onto the raft along with two other people and took the plunge down the ride's first drop. It was as the raft and it's passengers ascended the incline before the second drop when devastation occurred. The raft was going so fast, even with three people on it that as it reached the apex of the five-storey climb, it left the slide and became airborne. The two women on the ride suffered a broken jaw, a facial bone fracture and severe cuts between them, injuries that required dozens of stitches. But 10-year-old Caleb died. As the raft left the track and launched into the air, his head hit the metal support used to (ironically) hold safety netting in place, which decapitated him. His body landed back on the slide and continued along the ride, being pushed by the water, down its second drop and came to rest in the pool at the end. Witnesses claim to have seen so much blood that it looked like something out of a horror film.

An inquest revealed that Caleb Schwab had been allowed to sit at the front of the raft instead of in the middle, between the two adults, which led to an uneven weight distribution of the raft and this is what caused the raft to leave the slide. Schlitterbahn Kansas City Waterpark was closed for several days while an investigation into the accident was launched. The park reopened but Verrückt was shut down for good and the popular water slide was dismantled in 2018.

THE RAVEN

No, I'm not about to recite Edgar Allan Poe's famous poem. But The Raven roller coaster found at Holiday World & Splashin' Safari theme park in Santa Claus, Indiana was named after the great man's work. On the 31st of May, 2003 a self-confessed roller coaster fan Tamar Fellner, 32 attended the park's annual 'Stark Raven Mad' event that celebrates the park's coasters and the ride's many fans.

Tamar Fellner and her fiancé queued up and waited to board The Raven coaster, which at the time had the reputation as one of the fastest, most intense and scary wooden coasters in the world. Its twists, turns and sudden drops mimic the flight of a raven. It's fans always suggest enjoying the ride at night to get the full effect. It was around 8:00 PM when Fellner boarded the ride with her fiancé, they got on the very last

51

row at the back of the train and sat down. The safety check was carried out and the train was given the all-clear the leave the station. However, during the ride, several witnesses claim to have seen Tamar Fellner virtually standing up as the coaster sped along the track and down its numerous drops. Then during the ride's sixty-nine-foot drop, Fellner fell out of the train and landed on the tracks.

The ride finished and when the train returned to the station, her fiancé, a ride operator and a fellow park guest who was a doctor on the same ride, all rushed back along to tracks to where Tamar Fellner had fallen out... But she was no longer on the tracks where she had originally landed. She had now fallen through the track and plummeted to the ground. Rushing to Fellner, the doctor administered CPR while waiting for an ambulance to arrive, but Tamar Fellner was pronounced dead en-route to the hospital.

The investigation into the incident revealed that there was nothing wrong with the safety restraints and that they were working perfectly fine. Also, that there were no mechanical deficiencies on the ride at all. Which meant the safety restraints must have been undone on purpose by Tamar Fellner herself and that she stood up to get a bigger thrill from the ride as it sped along the tracks and down its drops.

Now, there have been several similar stories in this chapter already, and more to come, of people messing with or undoing their restraints, ignoring safety procedures and so on that led to tragedy. So, it would be very easy to put that down to the fact the people involved in such incidents were stupid idiots, not thought of as possessing much in the way of intelligence maybe? But Tamar Fellner was different, she was a Harvard MBA so a highly educated and intelligent individual.

DISNEY PARK DEATHS

Disneyland is often cited as 'The Happiest Place On Earth', opened in Anaheim, California, in 1955 and was the first-ever Disney theme park. Today, there are twelve Disney parks split over six different Disney resorts around the world. Yet even in the world's most popular and famous theme parks, death, suicide and even murder lurk.

BOOK OF DEATHS

MATTERHORN BOBSLEDS

The first recorded death at a Disney park was in May 1964 at Disneyland, California. The Matterhorn Bobsleds is a fast steel coaster that is built into a replica of the Matterhorn, a mountain found in the Alps. Riders sit in a small bobsled-like car and the track twists and turns through the mountain before coming to a stop at an alpine lake at the base of the mountain. 15-year-old Mark Maples was riding the Matterhorn Bobsleds with a friend and as the ride reached the peak of the mountain before its big drop, Mark Maples' friend unbuckled the seatbelt and that's when Maples decided to stand up, he lost his balance and fell around eighty-foot to the lower part of the track. The teenager suffered multiple injures including fracturing his skull and ribs. Mark Maples was rushed to a hospital but died three days later from his injuries.

Then, twenty years later in 1984, a very similar incident occurred when 48-year-old Dolly Young rode the same ride. As the ride was approaching its finale, Dolly was thrown from the car that she was sitting in and landed on a different part of the track. At the same time, another bobsled car, which was speeding along the ride, hit her. Dolly Young's head and chest were pinned beneath the wheels of the car and she was dragged along the ride until it was stopped. Young died of her injures soon after. An investigation revealed that Dolly Young's seatbelt was unfastened at the time of the accident. But she was in the car alone at the time, so it was never discovered if the seatbelt failed or if she unfastened it herself.

MONORAIL

19-year-old Thomas Guy Cleveland didn't want to pay for a ticket to enter Disney Land in June 1966. He thought it would be best to try and sneak into the park and try to get in for free instead. Making his way to the perimeter of the park, he climbed the sixteen-foot-high security fence and dropped down to the other side. He was in the park grounds, but not in the actual park itself.

Cleveland then climbed onto the monorail track, intending to walk along the track to the park, before climbing down and gaining entrance for free.

It was a plan, just not a very good one. As he was on the monorail track, he was spotted by a security guard who began shouting at him to get off. The guard was not calling out to Thomas Cleveland because he was trying to sneak into the park, but because a monorail train was fast approaching. Cleveland spotted a fibreglass canopy under the track and jumped onto it for safety, so the train could pass over his head. However, the clearance wasn't enough. The train hit Thomas Cleveland at full speed and dragged him along the track for around forty-feet or so before stopping. Cleveland died instantly. The person who was tasked with cleaning up afterwards reportedly said that they had to 'hose the kid off the underside' of the train.

PEOPLEMOVER

In July 1967, Disney opened the PeopleMover at Disneyland. It's a slow-moving, automated, elevated train system used to... Well move people. Originally envisioned as a serious mode of public transport for the future. As the ride was automated, it meant that the trains used for the attraction were unmanned and continually moving.

It was August 1967, just a few weeks after the ride originally opened when 17-year-old Ricky Lee Yama ignored the safety warnings issued by the park. He tried to jump from one train to another as the ride passed through a tunnel. As he jumped, he slipped and lost his balance, falling onto the track and into the path of an oncoming train. Ricky Lee Yama was crushed to death by the train as it dragged him along the track. Because the ride was automated, there was no one around to stop it so, his dead body was dragged for several-hundred-feet before the ride was eventually stopped.

Then thirteen years later in June 1980, the exact same thing happened again. 18-year-old Gerardo Gonzales repeated history and tried to jump from one train to another as he entered a tunnel. Once more he slipped and fell onto the track and once more he was crushed and killed by the train.

SPACE MOUNTAIN

Found in the Tomorrowland area of Disneyland. Space Mountain is an indoor space-themed roller coaster taking its riders on a speedy journey through the stars. The ride is filled with themed lighting effects and images to give the impression you are travelling through the galaxy.

On the 14th of August, 1979, a 31-year-old woman rode Space Mountain, but when the ride came to the end, she struggled to get out of the car feeling very uneasy. Staff instructed her to stay seated, they planned on removing the train from the track via a special exit of the ride that is used specifically for maintenance, with the plan to attend to her there and away from the public so the ride could continue with little disruption. However, the ride operator was not told of the incident or the plan to remove the train from the main track. So they accidentally sent the train and the guest around the ride for a second time as if nothing was wrong.

When the train and its passenger returned to the station, the 31-year-old woman was barely conscious and was rushed to a local hospital. She fell into a coma and died a week later. The coroner's report said the death was due to natural causes when a previously undetected heart tumour had dislodged and entered her brain.

RIVERS OF AMERICA

The Rivers of America are found in the Frontierland area of Disneyland. Guests to the park can use specially designed and manned rafts to enjoy the waters and even travel to Tom Sawyer Island for an interactive experience.

In June 1973, two siblings hid on Tom Sawyer Island until after the park closed. 18-year-old Bogden Delaurot and his 10-year-old brother tried to leave the island after hours, only to find no rafts were running to take them back to the main part of the park. They decided to swim for it, but the younger sibling could not swim. So Bogden Delaurot attempted to carry his little brother on his back and set out across the water. They made it about halfway across when Delaurot began to struggle and went under the water. The younger of the two was spotted and rescued by a passing security guard, but Bogden Delaurot was nowhere to be found. His body was discovered the next morning.

In June 1984, 18-year-old Philip Straughan, after enjoying himself on

Tom Sawyer Island, decided he didn't want to wait for the designated transport to take him back. So he instead, he stole a motorboat from the island that was used by staff in case of emergencies. He attempted to make it back to the main park with his friend using the stolen boat. The pair had been drinking before arriving at Disneyland and the 18-year-old eventually lost control of the boat, it hit a rock and Philip Straughan fell into the river. His friend managed to make it back to shore and quickly raised the alarm with the staff of the park who immediately began to look for the missing teenager. Philip Straughan body was discovered around an hour later.

THE COLUMBIA

The Columbia is a full-scale replica of the famed Columbia Rediviva ship. Passengers can board the impressive vessel and take a relaxing, scenic journey around the Rivers of America. It was Christmas Eve, 1998 when a freak accident would result in death. Guests patiently waited as the ship docked ready to welcome aboard its next group of passengers for a serene and clam trip.

One of the ropes used to secure the ship to the dock tore free and with it a metal cleat. The rope and cleat flew through the air and struck three people. 30-year-old park employee Christine Carpenter was one of them who sustained only minor injures. The other two were husband and wife, 33-year-old Luan Phi Dawson and Lieu Thuy Vuong, 43 who were also hit by the flying metal. Lieu Thuy Vuong suffered only minor inquires but her husband was not so lucky. Luan Phi Dawson was rushed to the hospital but sadly declared brain dead two days later and his life support was switched off.

This incident was the first Disneyland death not attributed to negligence/stupidity of the guest and put down to poor ride maintenance and lack of supervision.

BIG THUNDER MOUNTAIN RAILROAD

It was the 5th of September, 2003 at the Frontierland area of Disneyland when thrill-seeking guests were readying themselves to ride, Big Thunder Mountain Railroad. A ride set in the wild west era and features a runaway mine train, steel coaster design that cuts through a picturesque mountain range. The train was at full capacity and speeding along the track and had just entered a tunnel when things went terribly wrong.

The axle holding the wheels of the train's locomotive came loose and jammed against the brakes. The locomotive derailed and flew into the air, smashing against the ceiling of the tunnel. The momentum meant the train itself kept moving along the track and under the airborne locomotive. So as it came back down, it landed on top of the first passenger car causing extensive damage to the train. Ten people suffered minor to moderate injures. But 22-year-old Marcelo Torres became trapped in the car and had to be cut free by paramedics. Suffering severe blunt trauma and extensive internal bleeding, Marcelo Torres later died of his injures.

Another death occurred on the ride in February 2017. This time at the Walt Disney World, Florida park. A 57-year-old man suffered a heart attack brought on by a pre-existing medical condition while riding Big Thunder Mountain Railroad.

AMERICA SINGS

Carousel of Progress was an animatronic attraction at Disneyland that showcased futurism and living through various technological advances in the 20th century via an all American family. The attraction worked on a rotating stage idea, the building had an outer ring of six seating areas where the audience would sit, connected by divider walls that revolved mechanically around the fixed stage in the centre. So the audience moved around the stage and each part of the stage would feature a different scenario. In 1974, Carousel of Progress was updated and redesigned as America Sings, an attraction that takes the audience on a journey through America's history using music, humour and of course animatronics. The attraction was changed, but the idea of the rotating seats around the static stage remained.

Just over a week after America Sings opened on the 8th of July, 1974, an employee working on the attraction tragically died. 18-year-old Deborah Gail Stone was working as a hostess for America Sings, she greeted the guests and ensured that they were comfortably sat to enjoy the show. Stone stood to the left of the stage as the guests entered and once everyone was ready, the outer ring carrying the guests began to rotate. Unfortunately, Deborah Gail Stone was standing too close to the area where the outer wall rotated and where the stationary stage was, and she was crushed to death between the two. Guests enjoying America Sings said they could still hear the young hostess' painful screams over the loud music being played, as she was slowly crushed to death between the rotating wall, with some guests thinking the screams were actually part of the show. Since the tragedy, the attraction had been redesigned with breakaway walls to prevent such a thing from happening again.

OTHER DISNEY EMPLOYEE DEATHS

Phantom Manor is a dark, haunted house attraction found in Disneyland Paris. Described as 'a fun-filled mystery with ghoulish ghosts and spirits.' On the 2nd of April, 2016 the body of a 45-year-old maintenance worker was discovered by his fellow collogues. It was reported that he had been working on the lighting for the ride and had died from accidental electrocution.

California Adventure was the second Disney park built in California after Disneyland. 36-year-old Christopher Bowman was working on the magic carpet for the Aladdin live stage show at the Hyperion Theater in April 2003. Christopher slipped and fell more than sixty-foot from a catwalk. He was rushed to hospital but failed to regain consciousness and died a month later in May.

Pirates of the Caribbean is one of Disney's longest-running rides. Since the success of the film's based on the ride and the popularity of the Captain Jack Sparrow character, Jack Sparrow has since become the mascot for the attraction and the entire Pirates of the Caribbean brand around the globe. An interactive, live-action sword fighting show was added, to be performed outside of the ride. On the 6th of August, 2009. In Disney World, Florida, the live action show was being performed when actor Mark Priest slipped on a wet patch. Priest suffered a broken vertebra and severe lacerations on his head. He was treated in hospital but died a few days later on the 10th of August due to complications from his injuries.

BOOK OF DEATHS

Disney's famed parades are a wonder to witness, full of fun, energy and world cherished characters. On the 11th of February, 2004, Javier Cruz, 38 was playing Pluto in the 'Share a Dream Come True' parade in Disney World, Florida. Just before the parade made it's way to the public area and while it was still behind the scenes, the foot of the Pluto costume got caught under one of the floats. The float could not stop in time and Javier Cruz was struck, pulled under the float and killed.

DISNEY SUICIDES

Epcot is Disney World's vision of the future with its many rides and attractions all themed around the advancement of technology. It is mostly famous for its golf ball-like structure that houses the Spaceship Earth ride. But on the 12th of September, 1992 it would become a place of horror.

Allan Ferris, 37 entered the park after it had closed. When a security guard challenged him, Ferris pulled a sawed-off shotgun out from a bag he was carrying and shot at the guard. Two other security guards arrived at the scene and Allan Ferris shot at them too, miraculously missing all three of them. Two of the guards were taken hostage while the other managed to contact the police and raise the alarm. The hostages were held for around ten minutes or so in a bathroom before Ferris emerged from his hiding spot holding the sawed-off shotgun to his own chest. By then, several police officers had gathered to try and calm the situation, but Allan Ferris kept taunting the police to kill him, when they failed to do so, Ferris turned around as if to head back to the bathroom and his hostages. He put the shotgun to his head and pulled the trigger. Amazingly, he was still alive. The police wrestled the gun away from him while paramedics tried to save his life. Allan Ferris died while en-route to the hospital. But why did a man enter Epcot and kill himself?

Well, Allan Ferris had been in a relationship with an employee of the park. She ended their relationship citing domestic violence as the reason. Ferris had previously attempted suicide over the break up by slashing his wrists a few months earlier. So he entered the park and demanded to see his ex-girlfriend before putting the shotgun to his own head and pulling the trigger.

Disney's Contemporary Resort is a deluxe hotel found in Disney World, Florida. A beautiful and stylish hotel with shops, pools and it even has Disney's famed monorail running through it. In March 2016 an unnamed man climbed the resort's famous central A-frame tower and threw himself off, killing himself in full view of a busy hotel full of children. Guests were moved away from the area and the monorail system was shutdown while the scene was investigated and cleaned up.

TOMORROWLAND MURDER

The 7th of March, 1981 at the Tomorrowland area in Disneyland was a day no one could've expected. 18-year-old Mel Yorba was enjoying the many joys of the park. He began talking to a female guest, getting very flirty, but she was with her boyfriend, 28-year-old James O'Driscoll. The two men exchanged some harsh words and a fight broke out.

Mel Yorba began to run away and James O'Driscoll chased after him to the Tomorrowland area of Disneyland, where the conflict continued. More punches were thrown as guests looked on in shock. The fight escalated when O'Driscoll pulled out a hunting knife and stabbed Yorba twice, who then fell to the ground. An off-duty nurse rushed over to Mel Yorba and tended to his wounds. James O'Driscoll and his girlfriend attempted to leave the park but soon learned the exits were being covered by waiting security staff. So they decided to hide out in the park and try to escape later when it was closed, but they were discovered and handed over to the police.

At the time, Disney had a no emergency services allowed in the park grounds policy, as they felt it could ruin the atmosphere and 'magic' for visitors. Due to this, it took more than twenty minutes for a first-aid vehicle to arrive at the park and to where Mel Yorba lay dying in a pool of his own blood. And then another eleven minutes or so to get the wounded teenager to the park entrance where trained paramedics were waiting. By the time the first-aid vehicle made to to the awaiting paramedics, Mel Yorba had died of his injuries. James O'Driscoll was found guilty of the murder and sentenced to sixteen years in prison. After the fatal stabbing, Disney changed its policy on having emergency services in their parks and hired a professional private ambulance service for all Disney parks around the world.

VIDEO GAME DEATHS

I'm a big gamer and have been for many years now. Video games can get a bad reputation and are often blamed for some pretty terrible atrocities, such as school shootings and the like. I personally don't believe playing games can make a person violent. But sometimes, games are the backdrop to some pretty horrific, shocking and even stupid deaths that I just have to cover in this book.

PRIUS ONLINE

The fantasy, massively multiplayer online role-playing game, *Prius Online* was extremely popular, especially in its country of origin, South Korea where it attracted hundreds and thousands of regular players. Two of the game's fans were a 41-year-old man and a 25-year-old woman who met in an online chat-room and married soon after. The couple then went on to have a baby in 2010. Their baby had been born premature, which in Korean culture is seen as taboo and this deeply affected the new parents.

The couple began to feel shunned by society and they eventually lost their jobs. So they both found solace in *Prius Online* and would often spend hours and hours at a local internet café playing it. In the game, the couple made themselves a fictional life and even had a virtual avatar offspring called Anima, which they would care for in the game like a child. However, while they lost themselves in a virtual world looking after a virtual child, their very real 3-month-old daughter was left home alone and would very occasionally be fed some powdered milk between her parent's lengthy gaming sessions.

In September of 2010, the couple came home early one morning following a twelve-hour, overnight gaming session at their favourite internet café, to find their baby daughter lying in her crib, lifeless. An autopsy on the 3-month-old revealed she had been severely malnourished and had died of starvation. Investigating police officer, Chung Jin-Won said of the case that:

"The couple seemed to have lost their will to live a normal life because they didn't have jobs and gave birth to a premature baby. They indulged

61

themselves in the online game of raising a virtual character so as to escape from reality, which led to the death of their real baby."

The couple fled to the wife's parents house but were soon tracked down and caught by police. They both stood trial for the death of their daughter via neglect. The father was given the very lenient punishment of a one-year prison sentence, while the mother was given a suspended sentence. Pretty paltry punishment considering that a 3-month-old baby died. This story was used for the 2014 feature-length documentary, *Love Child* and was shown at the 2014 Sundance Film Festival.

ONLINE GAMING DEATHS

Online gaming can be a real minefield full of abusive idiots calling your mother all sorts of names, it can also be used for good to help raise money for charities, for instance, others just enjoy playing games with friends. But one thing the following tales all share in common is that online gaming can also kill.

In 2015, a 32-year-old Taiwanese man known as Hsieh, entered an internet café to play his favourite online game on the 6th of January. On the 8th of January, he was found in his chair, slumped over the computer he was using. Hsieh was a regular at the internet café and would often spend days at a time there. The staff even said he would sleep in his chair never leaving his post in front of the computer. This is most probably why Hsieh was left undistributed. When the staff realised there was a problem, emergency services were called and he was rushed to hospital but was pronounced dead on arrival from cardiac failure.

That same year just a few days earlier and also in Taiwan, another death in a different internet café occurred. This one was on the 1st of January, 2015. A man called Chu, 38 was found dead in the establishment's bathroom. According to the manager, Chu entered the internet café and stayed there for five days straight. Chu would consume instant noodles and energy drinks while playing various games online, hardly ever leaving the computer. Occasionally he'd take small sleeping breaks while still sitting right there at the computer and would only leave his post to use the toilet. After five days, other customers of the internet café complained that someone was hogging the toilet. One of the staff members when to investigate and found Chu lying with his face down on the toilet seat. It was discovered that Chu suffered from liver disease and gall stones, his existing health issues combined with his poor diet of noodles and energy drinks plus his five -day gaming binge is what lead to his death.

Still in Taiwan. An 18-year-old man called Chuang booked a private room at an internet café to play his favourite game, *Diablo III* on the 13th of July, 2012. After he had been playing online for forty hours uninterrupted, a staff member checked on him. Chuang was found unconscious and slumped over in his chair, but he was alive. The staff member woke him up to check of he was okay, this was when Chuang stood up and began to walk. He took a few steps before collapsing and was pronounced dead on arrival at the hospital. His death was put down to being sat down for so long that it created cardiovascular problems.

Not all online gaming deaths are from Taiwan. In February 2017 Brian Vigneault was a 35-year-old living in Virginia Beach, Virginia. He was known for his generosity and planned on taking part in a twenty-four-hour long online gaming marathon, playing *World of Tanks*, to raise money for the Make A Wish Foundation charity. A very generous deed he had done before. The marathon was even streamed to a live audience who could pledge money to Brian Vigneault's good cause. He had been playing for twenty-two hours straight, just two hours short of his target when he stepped outside to take a quick cigarette break, but Vigneault never returned to his seat. While taking his well-deserved cigarette break, he suffered a massive heart attack and dropped dead. It was later revealed that Brian Vigneault died of a fentanyl overdose, possibly linked to the copious amounts of energy drinks he consumed while trying and stay awake.

HALO 3

Daniel Petric, 16 was a very typical teenager from Wellington, Ohio who enjoyed playing games as many kids his age did. His strict parents didn't mind him playing games, but they forbid him from playing anything violent. His father, Mark Petric even said he would confiscate any violent games if Daniel ever bought any. He was not allowed violent games in the house, but that didn't stop Daniel from playing them. It was while at a friend's house when he was first introduced to the *Halo* games and he became a big fan of them instantly.

Daniel decided to buy the latest game, *Halo 3,* shortly after it was released in September 2007 but he knew he had to keep it hidden from his strict parents. Daniel Petric managed to keep the game secret for several weeks until in October his mother, Susan, discovered her son playing the game and told her husband. His father Mark Petric was disappointed that his son went against his wishes of not playing violent games and so confiscated the game as he said he would, he then locked the game away in a safe, the same safe also contained Mark's 9mm Taurus PT-92 handgun.

It was about a week after *Halo 3* had been taken away from Daniel on the 20th of October, 2007 when he decided that he would take back his game. He stole the key for the safe and removed *Halo 3*… Along with his father's handgun. His parents were in the living room getting ready to watch a baseball game. Daniel walked up behind his parents who were sitting on the sofa in front of the TV and said:

"Would you close your eyes, I have a surprise for you."

Daniel then shot his father in the head. Miraculously, Mark Petric actually survived the shooting despite being shot in the head at close range. Mark later recalled how: 'his head went numb and he saw blood pouring down from his skull.' Daniel then turned the gun toward his mother and shot her in the head too, as well as shooting her arms, and chest multiple times, killing her instantly.

As his father was bleeding from the wound, Daniel attempted to make the incident look like a murder-suicide and placed the gun in the hands of his shot in the head father before saying:

"Hey dad, here's your gun. Take it."

Shortly after the shooting, Daniel's older sister, Heidi arrived at the house with her husband to watch the baseball game with her parents. Daniel Petric refused to let them in saying that their parents had been fighting. The visiting couple could hear Mark's painful groans coming from the house and forced their way in to find their parents and the bloody aftermath of the shooting. Heidi called the police but before they could arrive, Daniel Petric escaped in his father's van with the copy of *Halo 3* in the passenger seat. He was eventually stopped via a police roadblock and when he was arrested, Daniel as reported as saying:

"My Dad shot my Mom!"

He was still trying to make out it was a murder-suicide. Daniel Petric was found guilty of the murder of his own mother and the wounding of his father (who amazingly made a full recovery), he was sentenced to serve a minimum of twenty-three-years in prison.

GRAND THEFT AUTO

It would be almost impossible to do a chapter on video game-related deaths and not do a *Grand Theft Auto* related story. The game series has been draped in controversy since it's original release in 1997 and is often the favourite scapegoat of the media for blaming violent acts. Many of the stories involving violence surrounding *Grand Theft Auto* are mostly over-exaggerated and often later proven to be false, but at least one of them was not.

2002 saw the release of the then-latest game in the long-running and hugely popular franchise with *Grand Theft Auto: Vice City*. In 2003 Devin Moore, who was 18 years old at the time and from Fayette, Alabama, was arrested after stealing a car and was taken to a local police station. While at the police station, Moore managed to grab the 40-calibre Glock automatic handgun of officer, Arnold Strickland and shot him twice, one of the shots hit him in the head killing him. A fellow police officer, James Crump heard the gunshots and came running down a hallway to investigate. Devin Moore was waiting and as James rushed to the scene, Moore fired three more shots at the officer, one of which hit him in the head killing him. But despite killing two police officers, Moore was not done yet, as he attempted to make his escape from the police station. He continued to run down the hall to the nearest exit, Moore passed the door of an emergency dispatcher, Leslie Mealer who was sitting at his desk, unaware that two of his fellow police officers had just been shot and killed. Devin Moore stopped outside of the door and fired five more shots into the room, one of which hit Leslie in the head, killing him. Three police officers killed and all shot in the head for doing nothing other than their jobs.

After the triple murder, which only took around a minute, Devin Moore grabbed a set of car keys and ran out of the police station where he then stole a police car and made a run for it. He was soon recaptured in Mississippi and upon being arrested for the second time he reportedly said:

"Life is a video game. Everybody's got to die sometime."

Once in custody, Devin Moore confessed to the murders and said he killed the three men because he didn't want to go to jail for the car theft he had previously been arrested for. It was suggested that Moore had lost the ability to distinguish reality from the virtual world after playing *Grand Theft Auto: Vice City* for long periods, which he freely admitted to doing too. A legal case was bought against the game's developers, suggesting they were to blame for the triple murder, but it was soon thrown out of court. In June 2003, Devin Moore was found guilty of the murderers and in August 2005, he was sentenced to death by lethal injection.

FARMVILLE

Facebook can be a great way to connect with family and friends. It also plays host to numerous online games, one such popular game was *Farmville*. The game is a life-simulation, agriculture type thing where you oversee and manage a farm. Grow crops, harvest them, sell them on to earn money to upgrade your farm to produce more goods to sell. Rinse and repeat. It's not one of the deepest games ever made, but it was and still is very popular.

In October of 2010 Alexandra Tobias, a 22-year-old mother from Jacksonville, Florida become hooked on *Farmville* and would play it for hours on end, every day via Facebook. Tobias became so engrossed in the game that she started to neglect her 3-month-old son. The baby did what 3 month-old babies wanting some attention do, he began to cry a lot. Probably hungry, maybe just looking for some comfort from his mother. However, Alexandra Tobias was just too busy playing *Farmville* to tend to her crying baby, and so she just kept playing the game instead. The crying continued until Tobias had enough, she walked over to the baby's cot and picked him up.

Now, this is where any normal mother would gently rock their baby to sleep, feed or maybe even try to entertain them. Alexandra Tobias decided to do something else instead, she viciously shook the 3-month-old repeatedly. The baby continued to cry and Tobias put him back in his cot before taking a cigarette break… Seriously, she stopped to smoke a cancer stick. After she finished her cigarette, Alexandra Tobias returned to her still crying son and continued to shake him, much more violently than before. She reportedly said that during the second shaking, she thinks that the 3-month-old baby hit his head on something… Or more accurately, she caused him to hit his head on something.

Sadly, the baby died of it's injures. When originally questioned over the death of the infant, Tobias claimed the family dog knocked him off the couch and said that was how the infant had hit his head and sustained the injuries. After further questioning, she finally confessed to shaking the 3-month-old to death and pleaded guilty. Alexandra Tobias was sentenced to serve fifty years in prison for killing her own baby son.

XBOX DEATHS

The Xbox brand is a series of popular game consoles made by Microsoft, but these machines designed to entertain can also be the basis for death.

In 2006, 25-year-old Tyrone Spellman from Philadelphia, Pennsylvania was playing on his Xbox console when his 17-month-old daughter decided she wanted some attention from her father. He ignored her and carried on playing on his Xbox. The bored baby soon found something to play with, the power cord of her father's game console. She sat there tugging at the cable until the Xbox fell from sitting under the TV and crashed to the floor. The console broke and so did Tyrone's temper. He repeatedly punched his 17-month-old daughter and even threw her across the room which caused the toddler to suffer a fractured skull. The baby died of her injures and in an attempt to cover his tracks, Tyrone moved the little girl's body to another room of the house to try and disguise the fact he beat her to death with his own fists. He then claimed that she was playing on the sofa and fell off when questioned. Tyrone eventually confessed to the brutal murder and was sentenced to serve forty-seven years in prison.

22-year-old Darrius Johnson from Broward County, Florida used his Xbox as a murder weapon. It was April of 2013 and Johnson was discovered by police casually wandering the streets and bleeding from a stab wound. He was being sought after, in connection with a burglary earlier that day where the victim of the burglary claimed they had stabbed the intruder. While his wound was being treated in the hospital, Darrius Johnson confessed that he had killed his girlfriend, Monica Gooden. He was reported as saying:

"She's in heaven, I think I killed her."

Police officers went to check on Gooden where they found the front door left open and a trail of blood lead them to the bedroom of the apartment she shared with Johnson. Her body was found with multiple stab wounds and three knives which Darrius Johnson had used to stab his girlfriend multiple times. Despite the ferocious stabbing, Monica Gooden was still alive. This was when Johnson reached for his Xbox console and beat his girlfriend to death with it, which was also found at the scene covered in blood. But why was Gooden brutally murdered? Darrius Johnson, after confessing to and detailing the murder, claimed that Monica Gooden had control over his spirit and that he had to sacrifice his girlfriend because her zodiac sign was Taurus.

On the 1st of March, 2016, 19-year-old Ki-Jana Freeman was murdered by 30-year-old Benjamin Young. Freeman and his 17-year-old friend agreed to sell an Xbox console to Young. A meeting was arranged and the teen friends sat in a car, waiting to meet up to make the sale. As they sat in the car, Benjamin Young pulled out a gun and began shooting at the unsuspecting teens. The 17-year-old friend escaped with several injuries and was treated in hospital, but Ki-Jana Freeman was not so lucky and died from the shooting. Young was arrested, found guilty of the murder and sentenced to death in Colbert County, Alabama. It was believed that Ki-Jana Freeman had stolen the Xbox console he was selling two days earlier from a friend of Benjamin Young. Another man,

BOOK OF DEATHS

De'Vontae Bernard Bates was also sentenced to serve twenty years in jail for his involvement in the planning of the murder.

EVERQUEST

Shawn Woolley was a 21-year-old man who, according to his mother, Elizabeth, struggled with epileptic seizures, learning disabilities, significant emotional and mental issues. Despite his troubles, Woolley landed himself a job and even moved into his very own apartment in Wisconsin. He was doing great on his own, even if only for a while at least.

It was Thanksgiving of 2001 when Elizabeth would find her son dead in his apartment. Shawn Woolley had quit his job the week before he was found dead. Falling into a pit of deep depression, he found the game *Everquest* as a source of escapism. He slowly but surely became addicted to the game over several weeks, in fact, it was even suggested the reason he quit his job was so that he could spend as much time as possible playing the game he soon became addicted to. The very same week that Woolley decided to quit his job, he also went out and bought a gun, unbeknown to his mother. A few days later and Elizabeth decided to pay a visit to her son at his apartment on the morning of Thanksgiving, 2001. She managed to force her way into Shawn Woolley's apartment after believing something was wrong when he failed to answer the door.

As Elizabeth walked through her son's apartment, she had a feeling of unease, a feeling any mother will tell you means something was not quite right. She made her way to the room where she knew her son would spend most of his time at his computer playing his favourite game. Elizabeth opened the door to find the place littered with takeaway food boxes and copious handwritten notes about *Everquest*. Still seated at his computer was Woolley, dead from a fatal gunshot wound to his head, his computer was still on and the game, *Everquest* was still running. It's still unknown exactly why Shawn Woolley decided to take his own life that day. But it must have been pre-planned and not an impulse decision as Woolley had purchased the gun the week before his suicide. Elizabeth Woolley always blamed the game for her son's continual depression and eventual suicide.

S. L. PERRIN

THE NINTENDO Wii

The staggering success and demand of Nintendo's latest console, the Wii, released at the end of 2006, was insane. Its ease of use and the fact it was specifically designed to be accessible to any and everyone meant it became a huge seller all over the globe. Those massive sales eventually led to stock shortages around the word with shop shelves continually being empty of Nintendo's latest games machine. Some consoles were being sold and bought for extortionate amounts on eBay via scalpers (does this sound familiar to any PS5 fans?). The much in demand console also gave birth to a KDND-FM radio competition in Sacramento, California on the 12th of January, 2007 which killed one of its contestants.

Jennifer Strange, 28 was one of several people who took part in KDND-FM's 'Hold Your Wee for a Wii' contest, wanting to win one of the popular consoles for her three children. The name of the competition really says it all, contestants were required to drink as much water as they could while not going to the toilet and without urinating. The contest was held at KDND's studios with around twenty people taking part. Contestants were given ever-increasing amounts of water to drink at fifteen-minute intervals. If they didn't drink all of the water when requested, they were out of the contest. If they had to the toilet or even wet themselves, they were out of the contest. Jennifer Strange managed to last several hours and she even made it to the final two contestants, with victory in sight. However, Strange had to bow out after suffering a pain in her stomach that kept growing increasingly worse and worse.

After leaving the radio station's studio, Jennifer Strange called a co-worker and told them that she was going home as she felt seriously ill and was in extreme pain. The co-worker then called Strange's mother who went around to check on her daughter, only to find her dead on the floor. Jennifer had died of water intoxication. The radio station in question came under heavy fire for the dangerous contest that ended up killing 28-year-old Jennifer Strange. The crew that came up with the idea for the contest in the first place were sacked and the morning radio show that aired the competition was pulled from the air. KDND-FM eventually closed down in 2017.

70

BOOK OF DEATHS

THE LEGEND OF MIR 3

In 2005, the online role-playing game, *The Legend of Mir 3* became the subject of one of the most bizarre and twisted game-related murders ever. Two Chinese players, Zhu Caoyuan, 26 and Qiu Chengwei, 41 were both in the same game together playing online. Chengwei owned a rare in-game weapon, a sword which he lent to Caoyuan to use. However Zhu Caoyuan didn't just use the weapon in the game, he sold it on eBay for real-world money, 7200 yuan (around £470). When Qiu Chengwei learned his friend had sold his virtual, in-game (not real) property, he became very upset.

First, Qiu Chengwei reported the 'theft' to the police. However, the police just told him that, as the item was virtual property and didn't really exist outside of the game, there was no case to be brought against Zhu Caoyuan. So he decided to take matters into his own hands and instead, he went to see the virtual thief at his home. When confronted, Caoyuan promised to hand over the money he made selling the non-existent sword to Chengwei. But an enraged Qiu Chengwei stabbed Zhu Caoyuan in the chest multiple times with what was described as 'great force' by the police, one of the wounds was a direct stab to the heart and killed Zhu Caoyuan instantly. Qiu Chengwei was given a suspended death sentence for the murder over an item that didn't even really exist.

WORLD OF WARCRAFT

One of the biggest and most popular online games is the mighty *World of Warcraft*. In 2014, *World of Warcraft* boasted a very impressive one hundred million registered accounts and by 2017, the game grossed over $9.23 billion in revenue. As I said, *World of Warcraft* is huge. With so many players registered to the game, of course, there are a few stories that do not end well.

13-year-old Zhang Xiaoyi from China was one of the millions upon millions of people who regularly played *World of Warcraft*. He was a very hard-working student at his school where he would often receive excellent grades. When he wasn't working hard at school, he would unwind and play his favourite game. It was the 27th of December, 2004 when Zhang Xiaoyi took part in a non-stop, Thirty-six-hour session on the game at an internet café after which, he went home as normal. However, instead of spending time with his loving family, the teenager made his way to the top of the twenty-four storey building he lived in and threw himself off. Zhang Xiaoyi left behind a suicide note stating how he:

"Wanted to join the heroes of the game he worshipped."

Rebecca Colleen Christie of Las Cruces, New Mexico was another fan and keen player of *World of Warcraft*, she would often play for hours on end losing herself in the game. Now there is nothing wrong with investing time in games, but when you have other responsibilities like raising a child, your gaming time needs to be managed. Sadly on the 26th of January, 2006 Rebecca Colleen Christie went to check on her 3-year-old daughter to find her limp and unconscious and so she called the emergency services. But sadly, the toddler was pronounced dead at the scene. An investigation into her death revealed that on the day her daughter died, Christie had been playing *World of Warcraft* for around fifteen hours non-stop. But one day of neglect would not be enough to kill a 3-year-old. Further investigation showed that Christie would spend day after day, for weeks and months, playing the game and not looking after her daughter, who died of malnutrition and dehydration. The 3-year-old's autopsy found cat food in her body, which suggested the child was often starved so much that she would have to eat the food put out for the pet. Rebecca Colleen Christie was sentenced to twenty-five years in prison.

Wii FIT

Wii Fit was a game developed for the Nintendo Wii console to help promote fitness. Using motion controls and a hardware peripheral called a Wii Balance Board, which tracked the user's centre of balance and movements. Players would partake in various physical exercises following directions via the game which would record your progress and keep track of your fitness level. It was like having your very own fitness instructor in the room with you. The game was so popular that *Wii Fit* was used in health clubs and gyms around the world and it was also used in nursing homes to help improve posture and fitness in the elderly. It's a game that has been used by young and old all over the world to keep themselves fit and healthy. On the 4th of March, 2009, Tim Eves, 25 was playing *Wii Fit* with his girlfriend at home in Hopton-on-Sea, Norfolk. Eves was taking part in a jogging exercise when he just suddenly slumped to the floor. His girlfriend immediately called an ambulance to rush him to the hospital, but he was pronounced dead on arrival. Tim Eves was a perfectly normal and fit 25-year-old with no previous medical conditions, so there was no real reason for why he suddenly died as he did. The death was put down to Sudden Arrhythmia Death Syndrome, a condition which causes the brain to become deprived of blood when the heart stops pumping blood.

BERZERK

If there is one thing all the stories in this chapter share in common so far, other than just being gaming related that is, it's that all the deaths are fairly recent and from 2000 onwards. But there was a much earlier gaming death that even spawned an infamous urban legend among gamers around the world. *Berzerk* was a classic arcade game released in 1980. It's probably most famous now for it's Evil Otto character that has gone on to be the basis for the previously mentioned urban legend. The legend goes that if you get a high score in the game and are killed by the Evil Otto character in the game, then the smiley face Evil Otto character will actually kill you in real life… As I said, it's an urban legend, but there is some grain of truth in the myth.

19-year-old, Jeffrey Dailey of Virginia was the first-ever supposed recorded death related to video games back on the 12th of January, 1981. Reportedly, Dailey suffered a heart attack after playing *Berzerk* and died… Except it never actually happened. It's fiction, I've checked and double-checked too. As far as I can tell, no one called Jeffrey Dailey of Virginia died in 1981 after playing any games at all, never mind *Berzerk* specifically. Yet the story of Jeffrey Dailey (that didn't happen) is believed to be what kick-started the whole urban legend to begin with. But just because the fictional Jeffrey Dailey didn't die playing the game, that doesn't mean no one didn't actually die after playing *Berzerk*…

On the 3rd of April, 1982, Peter Bukowski, 18 of South Holland, Illinois went into Friar Tuck's Game Room to play some video games. He was instantly drawn to *Berzerk* and dropped a few coins into the machine. He played a couple of games and got himself a high score, he put his initials into the game and decided to play another game. Once more, he got a high score and once more he put his initials into the game. Proud of his gaming achievement, he then stepped away from the arcade cabinet, turned around and took a few more steps before collapsing. One of the workers at the arcade rushed over and began to perform CPR while an ambulance was called. Bukowski was rushed to a hospital where he was pronounced dead on arrival. It was later revealed that Peter Bukowski suffered from a previously undiagnosed heart condition called Arrhythmogenic Right Ventricular Cardiomyopathy and that he had even suffered an unnoticed mild heart attack a few weeks before visiting the arcade and playing *Berzerk*.

There's a little additional that could also explain what agitated his heart condition. As, in order to get to the arcade to begin with, Bukowski walked a round trip of just over four miles, before he even set foot in the building, plus he stopped off to call on friends who came with him to the arcade. It had been snowing heavily too and it has been suggested that the four-mile walk in the snow could've aggravated Bukowski's undiagnosed heart condition. In fact, the friends he was with at the time noticed that Peter Bukowski was struggling to breathe properly after the walk when they arrived at Friar Tuck's Game Room.

Then, six years later, another *Berzerk* linked death occurred with a very strange and bizarre coincidence. It was the 20th of March, 1988 when Edward Clark Jr., 17 walked into Friar Tuck's Game Room... The very same arcade that Peter Bukowski was in when he died in 1982. Edward and his friends walked around the arcade looking to find some games to play. They spotted the *Berzerk* arcade machine... The exact same one that Peter Bukowski played shortly before he died. Sitting on the cabinet were a few coins that someone seemingly had left there. So Edward took one of the coins and put it into the arcade machine and played. This was when Pedro Roberts, 16 stepped forward and claimed the coins were his and that Clark Jr. now owed him for the money he had spent. Threats were made and an argument began before a fight broke out between the teenagers. A staff member had to separate the brawling teens and decided to kick them both out of the arcade. Knowing that kicking them both out at the same time would be a bad idea, the staff member told

Roberts to leave first and then waited around ten minutes or so before ordering Clark Jr. to leave and telling him to walk the opposite way that Pedro Roberts had gone earlier... Advice Edward Clark Jr. didn't take.

As Edward Clark Jr. and his friends walked along the street and though a car park, they didn't know that Pedro Roberts had been hiding and waiting in an alley, wanting to continue the dispute. As Clark Jr. and his friends strolled past, Roberts jumped out from his hiding spot, rushed toward his victim and plunged a knife into his chest. Edward Clark Jr. was bundled into the back of his friend's car and driven to the hospital but he died en route. Pedro Roberts was convicted of the murder in 1990 and was sentenced to an eleven-year prison sentence.

DARWIN DEATHS

In 1859, Charles Darwin came up with his theory of evolution by natural selection. In short, it is the principle by which, each slight variation of a trait, if useful, is preserved and so, uselessness and stupidity are eventually eradicated. People can die for some really inane reasons and this chapter celebrates Charles Darwin's theory of natural selection by looking at some of the many stupid and idiotic ways that people have lost their lives, due to their own lack of a half-decent IQ.

THE AUTOBAHN

Germany's Autobahn is famous for one very specific reason, the fact there are no speed limits for the most part. This gives drivers the freedom to drive as fast as they like and the Autobahn is often used to race cars and bikes from all over the world, it's become a bit of a tourist attraction for speed freaks. Of course, speeding vehicles can also be very highly dangerous, something 22-year-old Dean Steele should've been fully aware of.

It was in 2017 when Dean Steele was in Gudow, Germany with friends celebrating a birthday. Having just watched his football team win a match in a local pub and after more than a few beers, Steele and his friends were in high spirits. They thought it would be a good idea to get on the famed Autobahn, not in a car but on foot. Now the Autobahn is really busy and very dangerous during the day, but even though it's quieter at night, that danger is much, much worse as the drop in traffic gives eager drivers more chance of achieving higher speeds. So, of course, it was night time when Dean Steele and his friends decided to set food on one of the most dangerous roads in the world. They were all busy taking selfies on their phones as multiple vehicles tore past them at speed. After a short time of the friends displaying their stupidity, an Audi A6 driven by a 73-year-old man hit Dean Steele and killed him instantly.

THE PARTY DRINK

Parties can be fun. Food, drink and friends and more drink. In 2012 Gary Allen Banning, 43 was at a friend's house attending a party in North

Carolina where the music was playing and the drinks were flowing freely. Banning was in the kitchen when he spotted a jar with a golden liquid inside it. He grabbed the jar and took a huge swig of the liquid thinking it was a party cocktail... It wasn't. Earlier that day, the host of the party had been working on their car and gotten grease over their hands and used gasoline to clean themselves up. It was that same gasoline that Gary Banning took a swig of.

He dropped his head and spat the liquid out, all over his own clothing, down his chest and legs. Everyone that witnessed the incident had a good laugh, as drunk people at parties tend to do when someone does something really, really stupid. Now, what a logical thinking person would do after swigging and spitting out gasoline over their clothes is to get washed up and change that highly combustible party wear... That's not what Banning did. Instead, he thought it would be a good idea to have a cigarette. He took out a cancer stick, not that getting cancer would be an issue for him, and pulled out a lighter. After which, the inevitable happened and he went up in flames, Gary Allen Banning was rushed to hospital with severe burns but died a few days later.

THE WINDOW

Garry Hoy, 38 was a partner at law firm Holden Day Wilson LLP in Ontario, Canada. Hoy had a party trick that he was very proud of, he liked to prove the strength of the windows in the offices where the law firm resided. He would back away from his window of choice as much as he could, then run at full speed, throwing himself full-force into the glass and bounce back off it. Therefore proving just how strong the windows were. A trick he had pulled off many times in the past. In 1993 Garry Hoy wanted to do his party trick to impress a small group of visiting law students. The last time he would ever do his favourite stunt.

There was a moderate gathering of people on the 24th floor of the offices, not just the students he wanted to impress, but also several of his work colleagues who had seen his talent for running into windows multiple times before. Now with his audience watching, Gary Hoy began his run at one of the office windows. He slammed into the glass and bounced off it, much to the amusement of everyone watching and proving yet again that the windows were indeed unbreakable as he had done so many times before. But Hoy was not satisfied with just one demonstration. Full of confidence, he wanted another go, so he took another run and once more slammed into the glass and once more it did not break... This time the window popped out from its frame and it fell twenty-four storeys to the ground, quickly followed by Gary Hoy, who died on impact when he landed in the courtyard below. It's not known if the window broke when it hit the ground or not.

THE PROPHET'S DEATH

2015 in Zimbabwe, a self-professed Prophet called Shamiso Kanyama took part in a ritual that would end his life. Five local men came to Kanyama for help and guidance after several mysterious deaths within their family in a short space of time. The asked for their home to be cleansed of any evil spirits which they believed were causing the deaths. Of course, Kanyama was more than happy to oblige and tuned up at the home of the family ready to perform a healing ceremony. But before he could continue, he began to dig a hole in front of the house.

Asking for help with the digging, the members of the family soon joined in. After all the work, they had dug a decent hole. Shamiso Kanyama climbed into the hole and asked to be burred alive, claiming that this was the only way he could gain more healing powers needed to ward off the evil spirits. Kanyama then lay face down in the freshly dug grave and ordered his followers to cover him with the soil. One sensible person did step forward to try and stop the live burial, but Shamiso Kanyama claimed that the man was 'disturbing his angels' and urged his followers to continue filling the grave, promising that he would be dug up alive and well-armed with the powers to destroy the evil spirits haunting the house. Of course, that's not what happened as when Shamiso Kanyama was finally dug back up, he was dead. He'd quite literally dug his own grave.

NO CRASH HELMET REQUIRED

Wearing a helmet while on a motorbike is law pretty much around the world and a standard safety rule, much like wearing a seatbelt in a car. 55-year-old Philip A. Contos was one of a five-hundred and fifty strong motorcyclist group who was taking part in an anti-helmet rally in

BOOK OF DEATHS

Syracuse, New York, 2011. The rally was to speak out for having the right to riding a bike without a helmet as the protesters felt being forced to wear a helmet impeded their 'freedom' as bikers.

During the anti-helmet rally, one of the bikes in front of Contos stopped suddenly and he had to react. Contos slammed on the brakes of his bike and lost control of the 1983 Harley-Davidson he was riding which began to fishtail wildly. Philip A. Contos ended up being thrown over the bike's handlebars. Flying through the air, he hit the pavement head first and suffered terrible injures. He was taken to a nearby hospital but was pronounced dead soon after arrival. The doctor who examined and treated Philip A. Contos said that he would've easily survived the accident if he had been wearing a crash helmet instead of protesting against wearing one.

THE RELIGIOUS IDIOT

People are free to believe in whatever they want, as long as it harms no one and is legal of course. But sometimes, religious belief can lead to death. It was 2015 in a small town in Kentucky where pastors of a Pentecostal church would carry out their sermons using live venomous snakes. Their belief was that God protected them from the dangers of the snakes. They even had a strict policy in place that prevented anyone bitten by one of the highly venomous snakes from receiving medical attention, cos that's smart right? As they believed so deeply that God would save them from any deadly bites.

One of the church's pastors, John David Brock, 60 was delivering a sermon to his flock when one of the snakes bit him on the arm (what a shock). Instead of doing what any normal person would do and immediately go to the hospital for help and medical treatment… Cos you've just been bitten by a highly venomous snake, John just went to his brother's house instead and fell asleep on his couch because God would protect him as he believed. Of course, John Brock died due to the very painful and venomous snake bite, maybe God was having a day off that day? Even worse is the fact that the church still continues the practice of using live venomous snakes despite the fact it has already killed at least one of them. I guess there's just no cure for stupid?

S. L. PERRIN

THE (NOT SO) IMMORTAL PSYCHIC

Theprit Palee, 25 was a psychic from Thailand. He amassed plenty of followers and believers over the years and would often perform a traditional folk dance called 'Fon Pee Mot'. The dance is said to honour the ghosts of their ancestors. Palee claimed he was immortal as part of the dance involved his stabbing himself in the heart with a fake sword that would snap when forced into his chest. Which would supposedly prove that God watched over him and that he was immortal to his many followers… Remember, he used a fake sword to fool his followers and that he had done so many times previously too.

In 2017, Palee was performing the traditional dance in front of several of his loyal followers, he held the sword to his chest as he had done so many times before and plunged it into his heart. However, this time, the sword was not fake and did not snap, instead it pierced his chest and punctured his heart. He fell to the floor with blood pouring from the wound as emergency services were called. Theprit Palee was rushed to hospital but died of the stab wound soon after. You'd think a psychic would've known that was going to happen…

THE MAKESHIFT SLEDGE

Ski resorts can be a lot of fun, if you like sliding down a hill in the freezing cold, falling over a lot and drinking buckets of hot chocolate. In 2008, 46-year-old David Monk was enjoying a skiing holiday at a resort in Sauze D'Oulx in the Italian Alps with friends. They had been drinking… A lot. So they did what any idiots would do after drinking heavily at a ski resort, they decided to slide down a hill in the freezing cold.

Now, the slope they chose was closed at the time, but that slight inconvenience wouldn't stop Monk and his friends from having some fun, neither would the fact they didn't have any skis. A drunk David Monk and his equally drunk chums took a large foam safety mat that was tied around a metal barrier, to use as a sledge. Now, it's worth noting that you'd find these foam safety mats tied to all the metal barriers and posts on a ski slope, they are there for a very important reason, in case any skiers accidentally slam into them as they ski down

80

the hills. They help to avoid serious injury, they are called safety mats for a very good reason. Anyway, Monk and his friends climbed the slope with their makeshift sledge in hand ready to slide back down. They set off and began to pick up speed, sliding uncontrollably down the snowy incline and slammed into the very same metal barrier they stole the safety mat from. His friends suffered minor injures, but David Monk died instantly from severe head and chest injuries.

THE BUNGEE FLAWS

In July 1997 a man was taking a walk in Lake Accotink Park in Reston, Virginia when he found the body of 22-year-old, fast food worker, Eric Barcia at the base of a railroad trestle bridge in the park. Was it a successful suicide attempt, murder or million to one terrible accident that led to the death of the young man? Nope, it was just an act of sheer stupidity.

Barcia decided to have a go at bungee jumping but instead of going to a specifically trained and experienced bungee jump expert, he thought he could do it himself. Eric Barcia was aware the drop from the trestle bridge to the ground was seventy foot, so had pre-planned the whole thing in detail, he wasn't stupid, he had done his homework. Barcia had several bungees cords with him and tied them together, he then secured one end to the bridge and the other to his leg and jumped off the bridge. However, there were two very fatal flaws in Eric Barcia's bungee jump plan. The first flaw was that he didn't use a professional and safety checked bungee rope, he used several bungee cords, the kind of ones you use to secure bikes to the roof-rack on your car with the little hooks, that he just tied together. They may be fine for holding down some camping gear to your car, but they were nowhere near strong enough to hold the weight of a 22-year-old man plummeting seventy-foot. The other fatal flaw was that Eric Barcia made his makeshift bungee rope longer than the seventy foot drop. Okay, I was wrong, he was stupid then.

THE FORGETFUL SKYDIVER

Ivan Lester McGuire, 35 was a highly trained and very experienced skydiver, in fact, he was a regular at the Franklin County Sport

S. L. PERRIN

Parachute Center in Louisburg, North Carolina. McGuire had taken part in more than eight hundred skydiving jumps over the years both solo and with students. In April 1988, Ivan Lester McGuire took part in a skydive along with an instructor and a student.

McGuire's job was to record the skydive as the instructor jumped from the plane with the student securely strapped to him. Everything was going fine as the plane reached an altitude of ten thousand and five hundred feet. McGuire had the camera equipment strapped to his helmet ready to film the skydive as the instructor and his student readied themselves at the plane's door. Ivan Lester McGuire got the camera rolling and then after a brief countdown, the instructor jumped out of the plane along with his student and McGuire quickly followed them, all while filming the exciting action for prosperity. After a short drop, the instructor pulled his parachute cord to deploy his chute to bring him and his student floating safely to the ground. This was when Ivan also reached for his parachute cord and tried to deploy his chute… Only to realise he wasn't wearing a parachute, he'd just plain forgotten to put one on. Ivan Lester McGuire fell more than ten thousand foot and slammed into the ground at around a hundred and fifty miles per hour. His body was found later in a wooded area around a mile or so from the airfield where they took off.

THE KILLER LAVA LAMP

The lava lamp, an iconic staple of the sixties and seventies. These calming relics from the hippy movement are a joy to watch as the blobs of coloured wax encased in liquid and glass slowly move and bob around when gently heated via a heat-lamp in the base. They are designed to be soothing and relaxing… And especially fun if you've been 'experimenting' with substances that are not exactly legal… So I've heard. So how could something so serene and calming kill?

Well a 24-year-old man from Kent, Washington can prove just how lethal a lava lamp can be. In 2004, Phillip Quinn thought it would be a fantastic idea to heat his lava lamp by putting it on his stove and then cranking up the heat. Possibly thinking more heat would make the wax move faster, I don't know. Anyway, as the high and uncontrolled temperature of the liquid increased, so did the pressure inside the lamp

82

which steadily built and built until it exploded. Phillip was standing in front of the lamp when it blew up, sending extremely hot liquid, wax and shards of glass everywhere. One particularly large and sharp piece of glass flew through the air and toward Phillip Quinn, piercing his chest and heart which killed him instantly.

THE RABBIT HOLE

Rabbiting, the so called 'sport' of hunting rabbits. Rules and regulations vary from place to place in regards to rabbiting but it is perfectly legal in most places around the world. Hunters use a variety of methods to track and kill their prey including guns, ferrets and even dogs. Stephen Whinfrey, 50 had been rabbiting many times over the years and had gotten very good at it too. On New Year's Day, 2015, Whinfrey decided to go out to a local beauty spot in Doncaster, South Yorks to partake in his hobby, turn Elmer Fudd-like and hunt some wascally wabbits.

Around twenty-four hours later and Whinfrey's body was found. His dog was tied to a nearby tree pining for its owner. A couple of tied up bags were found near his body containing ferrets and digging equipment. Only his legs and torso were visible as Whinfrey had stuck his head into a rabbit hole in an attempt to catch himself a Leporidae. His body was found curled around the rabbit hole, as it seems he tried to push himself free with his legs. Scratch marks were also found on the ground around the hole where Stephen Whinfrey had been clawing at the soil as he struggled to release his head from the hole, He died of suffocation… And probably a few rabbit bites to the face too.

THE YOUTUBE PRANK

22-year-old Pedro Ruiz was an aspiring YouTube star who would often make videos where he would pull various 'pranks' on his girlfriend, Monalisa Perez and her on him in return. They would do silly but mostly harmless things, like hiding hot chilli peppers in each other's food or dusting a doughnut with baby powder, etc. Pretty much pointless and mostly harmless, but funny little pranks they would find amusing and then upload them to YouTube in hope that others would also enjoy them and make them internet stars. On the 26th of June, 2017 Monalisa Perez, who was only 19 at the time, Tweeted that she and Pedro Ruiz would do their most dangerous 'prank' yet, in an attempt to gain more viewers. Then around thirty minutes or so after that Tweet was made, Pedro Ruiz was dead.

Their funny 'prank' involved Perez shooting Ruiz with a .50 calibre Desert Eagle handgun, one of the most powerful and destructive handguns in the world. But of course, Ruiz thought it all out and had all the danger of a bullet speeding toward his heart covered, he had the idea of holding a book over his chest to work as a makeshift bulletproof vest. Now, bulletproof vests tend to be made from several layers of the very strong synthetic fibre, Kevlar, whereas books are made of paper... Not quite as strong and that's why they tend not to be used as bulletproof vests. Pedro Ruiz set up two cameras to capture his dangerous stunt. Monalisa Perez stood about a foot away from her boyfriend and squeezed the trigger. Needless to say, the .50 calibre bullet tore through the book and Ruiz's chest like a hot knife through butter, killing him instantly. The 'prank' video was never uploaded to YouTube but the shooting was witnessed by around thirty people who had gathered around at the time and yet, not one of them stopped to think that shooting someone with one of the world's most powerful handguns with only a book for protection was a bad idea? One of the witnesses was the 4-year-old daughter of the couple, oh and Monalisa Perez was heavily pregnant with their second child at the time too. She was jailed for six months after pleading guilty to second-degree manslaughter in 2018.

THE NIAGARA FALLS DAREDEVIL

The Niagara Falls, one of the most beautiful and awe-inspiring sights on the planet. Found between New York and Canada, the impressive waterfalls are made up of three separate and huge falls, the largest of which is called Horseshoe Falls. Over the years, Niagara Falls has attracted many people to carry out impressive stunts including tightrope walking and even just going over the beautiful but brutal falls in a barrel. Most of the stunts have been successful... Most.

On the 1st of October, 1995 California resident, Robert Overacker, 39 wanted to join the plethora of Niagara Falls daredevils and pull off his own unique stunt. Heading for the biggest of the three, Horseshoe Falls on his jet-ski and his home-made rocket-propelled parachute contraption.

BOOK OF DEATHS

His idea was to approach Horseshoe Falls at full throttle flying off the edge, at the same time he would trigger his rocket-propelled parachute, which he figured would launch him away from the mighty and deadly waterfall and he would glide gently to the ground bellow... Obviously, that didn't happen or he wouldn't be featured in this book.

Robert Overacker had seemingly thought of everything, except for one very basic rule. Water is wet. The heavy moisture of the famous Niagara Falls soaked his rocket-propelled parachute, so the rocket didn't go off and the chute didn't deploy when he pressed the button. At this point, he was already hurtling off the Horseshoe Falls on his jet-ski and it was too late to abort his stunt. He plummeted off the edge of the falls to his very wet death. His body was found by the famed Maid o' the Mist boat tours staff.

THE YELLOWSTONE HOT SPRING

Yellowstone National Park is a delightful and huge national park that spans an area of over three thousand, four hundred square miles. So vast is the park that it is found in three US states, Wyoming, Montana, and Idaho. Yellowstone features many lakes, canyons, rivers and even mountain ranges... Oh, and it's on top of an active volcano too. Well, according to the official Yellowstone National Park website, it's actually an active super-volcano under the park itself. One of the many popular features found in the park is its famous hot springs. What with there being a super-volcano lying under the surface of the park and all the heat that obviously generates, the hot springs are very, very hot. Slowly lowering yourself into a hot bath doesn't even compare.

The park is packed with huge warning signs telling people not to enter the hot springs as well as informing people of the fact that the whole area is geothermally active. Yet none of the many, many very clear warnings stopped 23-year-old, Colin Scott, from wanting to take an extremely hot dip. Scott was in the park with his sister, Sable on the 7th of June, 2016 enjoying the natural beauty the park offers, when he thought it would be a good idea to treat the volcanically heated springs as a backyard hot tub. The siblings decided to venture off from the designated and safe pathway and enter an unauthorized area near the Norris Geyser, which is the hottest, oldest, and most dangerous of

Yellowstone's thermal areas. Just to put things into perspective, a drill hole once measured a temperature of 459°F (237°C) in the same area. That really is quite very hot indeed.

Still, Colin Scott ignored all the warning signs and approached one of the springs in the hottest area of the park while his sister filmed him on her phone. Scott rested at the edge of one of the hot springs and reached down to test its heat, he then slipped and fell in. The alarm was raised and rescue workers came rushing to the scene but Scott was already dead, burnt to death via the extreme heat of the spring. An attempt to recover his body was called off due to a lightning storm in the area. The next morning and the rescue team arrived on the scene to resume the search, but Colin Scott's body was nowhere to be seen, it had literally been dissolved in the volcanic heated and acidic waters that are formed as the water rises through the ground via hydrogen sulfide in the rocks and soil (science!). Yellowstone's deputy chief ranger at the time, Lorant Veress was reported as saying about the incident that:

"In a very short order, there was a significant amount of dissolving."

THE BULLETPROOF CHARMS

Chinaka Asoezuwe, 26 was a native healer from Umuozo Ugiri, a small village in Nigeria. Locals would often seek him out for help with ailments and sickness remedies. In 2018 a villager, Chukwudi Ijezie visited Chinaka Asoezuwe seeking charms that would prevent bullets from penetrating his body… You can see where this is going, can't you?

After a while, the healer created the new 'bulletproof' charms and handed them to Ijezie, instructed him to wear them and stand in place, he then pulled out a gun so the charms could be tested. Naturally, Chukwudi Ijezie became very nervous and declined to be a test dummy. But so sure healer Asoezuwe was of his work, he wanted to prove the charms were indeed bulletproof and would prevent bullets from entering the body. So he placed the charms around his own neck and handed the gun to his nervous customer and instructed him to shoot. Needless to say, the bulletproof charms didn't quite work and cocksure healer Chinaka Asoezuwe died from the gunshot wound.

BOOK OF DEATHS

THE NOT SO CLEVER PROFESSOR

Alexander Zhankov, 44 was a Russian Professor working in the Ecology and Hydrology Centre of Oxford University. Like most Russian stereotypes, Zhankov enjoyed a drink or several. But going to the local pub for a few tasty, ice-cold liquid refreshments wasn't his thing. Instead, he liked to drink ethanol (basically pure drinking alcohol) directly from his lab supplies, which of course is highly dangerous. Zhankov's colleagues at the University showed great concern for his unsafe drinking habits, but he assured them that drinking ethanol was common in his homeland of Russia (is it?). So bad was his consuming of the dangerous chemical compound that Dr Ernest Gould, the centre's director said about the ethanol stocks that:

"Usage had risen markedly since the professor's arrival."

Professor Alexander Zhankov was also short-sighted and would often have to wear glasses. He wasn't wearing his glasses in October 2000 when he reached over to take a gulp of his favourite drink while working in his lab. Instead of downing his usual tipple of ethanol, he drank methanol... Which is still technically alcohol, only a lot more volatile and toxic than ethanol. Consuming as little as ten millilitres of pure methanol can cause permanent blindness. The highly educated professor downed several large mouthfuls of the highly toxic chemical, he then stumbled to the road outside of his lab coughing and spluttering before collapsing on the ground. He was rushed to the hospital and placed on life support, but it was turned off after it became very clear that Alexander Zhankov had zero chance of recovering. See, even highly educated professors can prove Charles Darwin theory right.

THE REALLY, REALLY STUPID CRIMINAL

Some criminals are highly intelligent and despite their nefarious ways, you can't help but admire their creativity and cleverness in carrying out some of their carefully planned crimes. That can not be said for 33-year-old David Zaback, who decided to pull off a robbery on the 3rd of February, 1990 in Renton Highlands, Washington. It was around 4:40 PM when he entered an establishment and pulled out a gun before declaring he was going to rob the place and if anyone moved or tried to stop him, that he would shoot them dead. An easy robbery with little risk using a classic method that is very well proven to be effective.

It was a basic plan and one that has worked many times in the past for others. See, it is the simplicity of why this kind of crime often works, as no one will risk their lives over a bit of cash from a shop-till. The shock of someone walking in brandishing a gun and screaming threats is enough to get people to do what you want them to workout question. However, there were a couple of slight issues with David Zaback's attempt at a classic hold-up robbery. One of the main problems was that the place Zaback tried to rob was a gun store, those places tend to be full of guns and gun owners who know how to use guns. Another problem was the fact there was a police officer in the store at the time of the robbery. In fact, witnesses claim to have seen Zaback walk around the clearly marked and hard to miss police patrol car that was parked at the front door of the gun shop to get into the building, to begin with. None of these huge warning signs put Zaback off as he fired a few rounds from his gun, only for the gun store worker, the police officer and several of the store's customers to return fire in defence.

Amazingly, no one was hurt in the gunfight... No one except David Zaback of course, who was shot three times in the chest and once in the arm. Paramedics were called to the scene but David Zaback was pronounced dead at the scene.

THE FIREWORK LAUNCHPAD

Devon Staples, 22 worked at Disney World, Orlando playing both the Gaston and Goofy characters... But this is no theme park death otherwise it would've been in that chapter. It was the 4th of July, 2015 and Staples was doing what a lot of proud and patriotic Americans do on that date, he was celebrating America's independence. Along with copious amounts of beer and food, fireworks play a big part in any 4th of July celebrations and this day was no exception.

Devon Staples was out with friends celebrating the 4th of July and decided to set off a few fireworks himself. During a party in the backyard of a friend's house, he picked up a rather large mortar tube styled firework and placed it on his head before lighting the touchpaper… Again, it was a large mortar tube firework, not some measly rocket. Of course, the firework did what fireworks do and exploded with a huge bang and an orgy of colours. Devon Staples was killed instantly, I mean, he did have an explosive device on his head. Cody, Devon's bother, who was celebrating with his sibling, but in a different part of the house where the party was held at the time said:

> "I was the first one who got there. There was no rushing him to the hospital. There was no Devon left when I got there, It was a freak accident. But Devon was not the kind of person who would do something stupid."

With respect Cody, I think trying to launch a highly explosive mortar-like firework from your head could be considered fairly stupid.

THE 'SHORT CUT'

26-year-old Cammie Krusoe won a radio contest for a pair of tickets to attend a Dave Matthews Band gig in September 2007. Excited Cammie invited her friend Megan Thompson, 28 to join her at the concert which was to be held at the Ford Amphitheatre, Tampa Bay, Florida. The concert was delayed due to a sudden torrential thunderstorm. So the two young women thought it would be best to head back to where they parked the car to get out of the downpouring of rain, wait for the storm to pass and the concert to begin. There was a slight issue with the fact that they didn't park in the lot of the amphitheatre itself, they parked around half a mile away at the Seminole Hard Rock Casino. So they thought it would be best to take a 'short cut' back to the car at around 8:30 PM in the middle of a huge thunderstorm.

Now, this 'short cut' would lead them over a hundred-yard grassy field that is now soaking wet and very muddy due to the weather, a very busy seven-lane interstate and then through a still under construction parking garage. That's before you include the numerous six-foot safety fences to keep people out and away from danger. Even then, if they managed to get through all of that, this 'short cut' would lead them to the back of the casino and they would then have to walk all the way around it to get to where their car was parked at the front. So a not so short 'short cut' all things considered… Oh, and they also had to pass several free shuttle bus services that had been put on specifically to transport people to and from the casino. Again, there were <u>FREE</u> shuttle bus services that would take them directly to where they needed to go, and they had to walk past them to take their planned 'short cut'.

So, the duo set out on their treacherous journey to reach their car in torrential rain at night. They made it across the drenched in rain, grassy and muddy field and then clambered over the first six-foot fence to keep people away from the busy seven-lane interstate. While trying to cross the very busy road, both Cammie Krusoe and Megan Thompson were hit by a fast-moving Toyota in the very first lane of the interstate, Cammie Krusoe was sent flying into the centre lane and was run over by a Ford, while Megan Thompson who was also knocked down into another lane by the Toyota, and was then run over by an Audi. Both of them died of their injures. If only there had been a <u>FREE</u> shuttle bus service that went from the concert to the casino where they were parked eh?

IRONIC DEATHS

Death can come in many different flavours and despite the end result of the loss of life, sometimes that result can leave a wry smile on the face. Especially when it seems like the Grim Reaper is a fan of irony.

ESCAPING A DEATH SENTENCE... FOR A WHILE

Michael Godwin (AKA Michael Anderson Sloan) was convicted of the murder and sexual assault of Mary Elizabeth Royem in 1983. He was tried and sentenced to death by electric chair in South Carolina. Whilst on death row and awaiting his inevitable demise by two thousand volts, his lawyer managed to successfully overturn the original punishment via an appeal. So his initial death sentence was reduced to life in prison instead, Godwin just escaped a literal death sentence.

While serving his time in prison, Michael Godwin became very well behaved, he even managed to earn two college degrees. Godwin hoped that his good behaviour would reduce his sentence even more so, and possibly that his good behaviour could even lead to him being released. His behaviour tied with the successful appeal via his lawyer is said to be why his electric chair death sentence was changed to a life in prison one instead. Still, he was a murderer and his weapon of choice was an electric iron. So, a killer using an electric iron to kill someone escapes the death penalty by electric chair is slightly ironic, but that not the real irony of this tale.

It was 1989 and now 28-years-old, while serving his life sentence in prison, Michael Godwin attempted to fix his broken earphones so he could use them to watch some TV. He was naked as he sat on the metal toilet in his prison cell and fiddled with the wires of his broken earphones... The earphones were still connected to the TV at the time too. He then placed the bare, exposed and live wires of his broken earphones into his mouth. The electric current from the TV flowed through the earphones, coupled with the moisture of his mouth where the exposed wires were, plus the fact he was naked and sitting on a metal toilet lead to Godwin being electrocuted to death in his cell. It may not have been the two thousand volts he escaped from via the electric chair, but even the smaller shock from the TV via the earphone wires entering his body through the mouth was enough to electrocute himself to death. He may have managed to escape death via the electric chair… But only for a few years.

REAL LIFE PSYCHO SHOWER SCENE

Alfred Hitchcock's film adaptation of Robert Bloch's *Psycho* novel is one of the greatest films ever made. The most (in)famous scene in the picture is, of course, the shower scene where young Marion Crane meets her demise at the hands of 'you know who' topped off by those iconic, ear-piercing violin screeches.

Myra Davis worked on the film as the body double of the film's star, Janet Leigh as well as providing the voice of Norman Bates' mother in the film. In 1988, she was raped and murdered by Kenneth Dean Hunt. Myra Davis, who was 71-years-old at the time, hired 22-year-old Kenneth Dean Hunt as a handyman to help do odd jobs around her Los Angeles home. Unfortunately, the handyman was massively obsessed with Hitchcock's *Psycho* movie and when he learned his employer was in the film as a body double for Janet Leigh… He wanted to re-enact that shower scene for real. Trying to force the elderly Davis into the shower so he could live out his sick fantasy, the plucky retired actress fought back, but her younger attacker overpowered and then raped and strangled Myra Davis to death. Kenneth Dean Hunt fled from the scene and even managed to elude police capture for many years, he was only caught and found guilty of the murder (and of several others) in 2001 when he was finally sentenced to life in prison.

But, there is a final twist of irony to this story. While Myra Davis did indeed work as a body double for Janet Leigh in *Psycho*… She never worked on the (in)famous shower scene at all. The body double for that particular scene was actually an actress called Marli Renfro. So the killer didn't even have the right actress for his deranged *Psycho* shower tribute. Even more so, papers at the time made the exact same mistake and were initially reporting on the death of Marli Renfro who was very much alive and well at the time, instead of the actual victim of the murder, Myra Davis. Both the killer and the press made the same mistake.

AN ALL TOO ACCURATE LEGAL DEFENCE

Clement Vallandigham was a respected politician and lawyer during the 1860s and early 1870s working in Lebanon, Ohio. His final case as a lawyer was representing defendant, Thomas McGehean who was on trial for murder during a bar-room brawl with another man in 1871. The defendant was accused of shooting and killing the victim, Tom Myers. But McGehean was adamant he never fired a shot and that Myers had actually shot himself by accident when trying to draw his gun from his pocket while standing up from previously kneeling down. The defence seemed rather weak and no witnesses could collaborate the defendant's story.

This was when Clement Vallandigham, 50 spoke to his fellow attorneys of the case and said he could prove that defendant's Thomas McGehean cries of innocence. Vallandigham came up with the idea of re-enacting the scene and placed an unloaded pistol in his own pocket. He then knelt on the floor just as the victim, Tom Myers was when he supposedly accidentally shot himself. Vallandigham followed the description of events to the letter and pulled out the empty gun from his pocket… Only it wasn't unloaded as he originally thought. The gun snagged on Clement Vallandigham's clothing and discharged, the pistol's ball baring bullet hit him in the belly and died the next day of peritonitis.

Yet, his defence demonstration actually worked and the jury acquitted Thomas McGehean of the murder charge and released him from custody… Only for him to be shot and killed just four days later.

COFFEE TABLE REVENGE

On the 23rd of September, 1988, Brenda Sue Schafer was brutally tortured and murdered by her abusive boyfriend, Melvin Henry Ignatow in Louisville, Kentucky. Schafer had finally had enough of the relationship and decided to end it, but when Ignatow found out, he took the break up very badly. Enlisting the help ex-girlfriend Mary Ann Shore, Ignatow and Shore kidnapped and took Schafer to Mary Shore's home, There, Brenda Schafer was blindfolded, gagged and tied to a glass coffee table, raped, sodomised and beaten before being chloroformed to death. While this sickening murder occurred, Shore stood there taking pictures and documented the whole thing. Ignatow and Shore then untied Schafer's bloody and brutalised body form the glass coffee table and buried it in the back garden of the house before cleaning up any evidence.

Now, Melvin Ignatow was actually put on trial for the disappearance and (believed) murder of Brenda Schafer, but due to a lack of evidence, no witnesses, no body and some supposed sloppy police work, he was acquitted of the murder charge. The judge presiding over the case was so embarrassed by the verdict and everything else surrounding the case that he actually wrote a letter of apology to Brenda Schafer's family. After the disastrous trial had ended, the photos taken by Mary Shore of the brutal murder were found and all the proof needed of Melvin Ignatow's guilt was discovered. Finally, the police had the man responsible for Brenda Schafer's horrific murder … But there was a slight problem. The legal principle of double jeopardy, a stipulation that prevents an accused person from being tried again on the same/similar charges following a valid acquittal or conviction. So even though Melvin Ignatow was guilty, the police knew he was guilty, and the fact they had evidence there as proof to convict him for murder, Melvin Ignatow just could not legally be tried for the same crime twice. So, he was put on trial for perjury instead and Ignatow even eventually confessed to the crime, detailing exactly what he did to Schafer, boasting about his actions, all while knowing he could not be convicted for the murder he was guilty of. Melvin Ignatow was sentenced to eight years for one instance of perjury nine more years for another. He was released from jail in 2006 after quite literally getting away with murder.

But, on the 1st of September, 2008, Melvin Ignatow was finally brought to justice for the murder by several sharp shards of irony. He was walking around his home when he tripped and fell face-first into a glass coffee table, a very similar table to the one that Ignatow used to rape, torture and then murder Brenda Schafer some twenty years previously. Suffering multiple lacerations to his head and arms and torso, Ignatow then tried to make his way to his bedroom where the telephone was, but he bled out before he could make it. His badly cut and bloody body was found by a neighbour.

BOOK OF DEATHS

POOL PARTY CELEBRATION

At the end of the summer period, the lifeguards of New Orleans always hold a big pool party, it's a long-standing tradition enjoyed for years. All public pools in the city are closed down at the end of July so the lifeguards of the 'Big Easy' can have some fun following the busy summer season. In 1985, they held a special pool party to celebrate zero deaths over the summer holidays. That year was the first time in memory that there had been no drownings, so they had a good reason to party more so than usual.

As the pool party wound down at the end of the night, the body of 31-year-old Jerome Moody was found at the bottom of the deep end of the New Orleans Recreation Department pool. Now, Moody wasn't a lifeguard himself, but you'd think that at a pool party held for lifeguards that at least one would've been there. In fact, around half of the two hundred guests at the party were certified lifeguards and four of them were even on duty at the time of the drowning. Yet after a zero death summer season, around a hundred lifeguards at the party, none of them noticed Jerome Moody drowning to death.

NIAGARA FALLS DAREDEVIL

Yeah, I know we had one of these Niagara Falls deaths in the Darwin Deaths chapter but a lot of people have died doing silly things over the famed falls. However, this one is a little different. Bobby Leach from Cornwall, England was the second ever person to go over Niagara Falls in a barrel and survive. He carried out his stunt on the 25th of July, 1911. While he lived, he suffered multiple injures including two broken knee caps and a fractured jaw.

After his successful Niagara Falls... Well fall, and after spending several weeks recovering from his numerous injuries, Leach became a big celebrity for the time. He would go on tours around the world, especially the US and UK, where he would hold talks of his feat and even pose for pictures with the barrel he used. His celebrity status lasted for a good few years, in fact, fifteen years after surviving the Niagara Falls. Leach went on a publicity tour of Auckland, New Zealand in 1926 still talking about his stunt and posing for pictures. One day and Bobby Leach was walking down the street when he slipped on a discarded orange peel. He only fell about five foot, which compared to the one hundred and eighty-odd foot drop of the Niagara Falls, really was not much or as dangerous. The fall caused an injury to his leg which became infected and Leach eventually developed gangrene. His leg had to be amputated in an attempt to save his life, but Bobby Leach died following complications soon after.

FAMOUS LAST WORDS

The Battle of Spotsylvania Court House was the second major battle of Lieutenant General Ulysses S. Grant's 1864 Overland Campaign of the American Civil War. On the 9th of May, 1864 Major General John Sedgwick was leading an attack against the Confederate army, Major General Sedgwick began by ordering his men to move and try to flank the enemy, but their movements were being hindered by constant sniper fire. Bullets whizzed by and some of his men dove to the floor to try and avoid being shot. This was when the Major General felt the need to berate his men by saying:

"What! what! men, dodging this way for single bullets! What will you do when they open fire along the whole line? I am ashamed of you. They couldn't hit an elephant at this distance."

Shortly after he ranted at his men, another soldier dove to the ground directly in front of John Sedgwick as another sniper bullet whistled past. The Major General tapped the lying prone man in front of him with his foot and said:

"Why, my man, I am ashamed of you, dodging that way."

He then repeated the remark:

"They couldn't hit an elephant at this distance."

Just seconds after finishing insulting his diving for cover soldier, a sniper bullet hit Sedgwick under his left eye. He then turned to one of his men standing nearby and blood began to spurt out from his left cheek. Major General John Sedgwick then fell forward and died from the wound.

PACK UP YOUR TROUBLES

Welsh songwriter George Henry Powell penned the lyrics to the song *Pack Up Your Troubles in Your Old Kit-Bag and Smile, Smile, Smile.* His brother, Felix Powell wrote the music. The song went on to win first prize in a World War I competition for the best morale-building/marching song. *Pack Up Your Troubles* is often claimed to be the most optimistic piece of music ever written and when you hear it, that's a hard opinion to argue against considering what was going on at the time. Both soldiers and civilians alike would sing the song to keep their mood high during one of the most bloody, horrific and deadliest wars ever witnessed. Even with the dead bodies mounting up, people would still gather around the piano and belt out the song down the pubs just to keep their own and other's spirits high.

Sadly, Felix Powell's massively uplifting song that gave hope, comfort and consolation to millions of people around the world during a bloody world war didn't really extend to him. Dressing up in his Peacehaven Home Guard uniform, he took hold of his standard-issue rifle, pointed it to his heart and squeezed the trigger. Powell committed suicide in the midst of World War II, 1942 while his song continued to raise the hopes of millions. It has been suggested that Felix Powell decided to end his own life as he was so depressed and couldn't envision an end to the war.

EVEN GOD CAN BE IRONIC

It was the 17th of January, 2012 and Ariane Noelle Patterson was celebrating her 21st birthday. Patterson was a student at Gardner-Webb University in Boiling Springs, North Carolina. In the morning, she jumped on social media to express her joy of life by Tweeting:

"Thank you God for another year of life."

To all of her followers on the morning of her special day and garnered several replies wishing her a good life and a happy birthday. Patterson then made her way to university where she was studying religion. It was just a normal day and everything was fine. After lunch, she returned to her religious class and suddenly collapsed. A fellow student who was a trained emergency medical technician began to perform CPR on Ariane

Patterson until paramedics arrived while other classmates began to pray for her life. Patterson was rushed to Cleveland Regional Medical Center but died soon after arrival. It was later revealed that Ariane Patterson suffered a heart attack from complications of systemic lupus erythematous and she had dropped dead after thanking God for her life.

FIT ENOUGH TO DIE

James Fuller Fixx, more famously known as Jim Fixx, was a fitness guru in the seventies and eighties. He is often credited with kick-starting America's fitness revolution, particularly when it came to running and jogging. Jim wrote several best selling books on fitness and running, he also made numerous TV appearances and even a fitness video in 1980 before they became the popular celebrity staple they are today. Running was not just a physical exercise to Fixx, it was a way of life. He was known to preach the idea that active people lived longer. Jim Fixx lived to jog and jogged to live.

On the 20th of July, 1984 when Fixx was 52-years-old, he headed to Vermont Route 15 in Hardwick, Vermont to partake in his favourite pastime of jogging. It was around 5:30 PM when a passing motorcyclist found Jim Fixx lying on the ground, the alarm was raised and he was taken to hospital but pronounced dead on arrival. An autopsy revealed that Jim Fixx had died of a massive heart attack while out running to stay fit to extend his life.

YOU ONLY LIVE TWICE

In Russia, 2011, 49-year-old Fagilyu Mukhametzyanov complained to her 52-year-old husband, Fagili that she felt rather unwell. She described how she was suffering from severe chest pains. The loving husband quickly rushed his wife to the doctor in their home-town of Kazan City, Russia. But by the time they made it to the doctor, Fagilyu had fallen unconscious. It seemed that she had suffered a heart attack and so the doctor pronounced her dead. Fagili decided not to have his recently deceased wife embalmed right away. He wanted to hold a celebration of her life first, with Fagilyu lying in rest the day after her death for family and friends to say goodbye before the funeral. A decision made in line with Fagili and his wife's religious beliefs.

BOOK OF DEATHS

A day later and Fagilyu Mukhametzyanov was placed in her coffin as her funeral was arranged so family and friends could pay their respects. As Fagili said his final farewell to his wife, joined by those close to him, she suddenly woke and sat up in the coffin. Looking around at everyone crying and praying, she soon realised where she was and screamed. Fagili Mukhametzyanov was taken to hospital but died (again) just a few minutes later as her husband Fagili remembers:

"Her eyes flapped. However she just lived for an additional twelve minutes in intensive care prior to her dying once more, this time permanently."

DON'T DRIVE TIRED

On the 22nd of July, 1998, a 77-year-old man was found dead in his car just north of San Diego, California. The car had hit a tree at speed, but at the time, it was not known exactly why the car left the road and hit a tree fast enough to kill the driver. After an investigation, the driver was identified as Eugene Aserinsky. In 1953, Aserinsky earned his PhD in physiology at the University of Chicago, when he produced his groundbreaking thesis: *Eye Movements During Sleep*. Basically, Aserinsky discovered rapid eye movement, or REM sleep and revolutionised sleep research forever.

The discovery of REM sleep proved that the brain is still active and even that it actually became more active during sleep and how it all connected to dreaming. His groundbreaking research into sleep patterns changed the world and Eugene Aserinsky became known as one of the major pioneers of sleep research, earning untold respect and adulation among his peers. His work has opened the doors on how people think about sleep, brain activity, dreams and everything connected to dreaming from 1953 onwards. His research is still used to teach medical experts and dream specialists today. As for the reason why his car crashed into a tree and killed him in 1998? There were no tyre marks to suggest he panicked and slammed on the breaks, the autopsy showed no indication he was tense as he died or that he was under any kind of stress. In fact, it is believed that Eugene Aserinsky, the sleep expert, actually fell asleep while he was driving.

S. L. PERRIN

THIRTEEN GUN SALUTE

John Kendrick was an American sea captain in the 1700s. He was an adventurous kind of chap as he commanded warships during the American Revolution and whaling ships during peacetime. He was a vastly experienced sea captain and very much respected among his peers.

On the 11th of December, 1794, John Kendrick's ship, Lady Washington and his men were in Honolulu, Hawaii (then known as Fair Haven) when an invading chief called Kaeo launched an attack to try and drive out the local Hawaiian chief, Kalanikupule from Honolulu in what would later be called the Battle of Kalauao. Teaming up with the crew form a British vessel, The Jackal and its captain, John Kendrick sent some of the men from both ships who helped to force the attacking party to retreat into the hills of Honolulu. From his ship, Kendrick spotted the retreating chief Kaeo and his men making a run for it, he fired the cannons of his ship in the direction they were heading to give away their location to the warriors of chief Kalanikupule on Honolulu. Kaeo and his retreating men were found and killed, putting an end to the battle and making chief Kalanikupule the victor.

The next morning on the 12th of December at around 10:00 AM, John Kendrick fired a thirteen gun salute from his ship's cannons in celebration of the victorious battle from the previous day and to show respect and solidarity toward the British crew of the Jackal who had helped. After which, Captain John Kendrick and some of his men settled down on the deck of their ship, Lady Washington to enjoy a well-deserved breakfast. At the same time, Captain William Brown of the Jackal returned the thirteen gun salute mark of respect for their new allies. Now, when a gun salute is carried out these days, blanks are used to create the sound but not risk injuring anyone, and that was pretty much the same back in the 1700s too. The cannons would be loaded with gunpowder to create the noise, but they wouldn't be loaded with ammo. Sadly, Captain William Brown didn't check his cannons before firing the salute as one of his guns was still loaded with grapeshot ammo. The projectile smashed into the deck of the Lady Washington, killing the celebrating and much respected Captain John Kendrick and his entire crew.

BOOK OF DEATHS

ANTI-SUICIDE BARRIER

San Francisco's Golden Gate Bridge is one of the most famous and recognisable bridges in the world. At one point it was both the longest and the tallest suspension bridge on Earth. It has been seen in countless movies and TV shows and has even been declared as one of the Wonders of the Modern World by the American Society of Civil Engineers. In short, it's an impressive feat of engineering and even claimed as being the most beautiful and most photographed bridge in the world, ever! Yet despite its fame, or perhaps due to its fame, Golden Gate Bridge is one of the world's most notorious suicide spots.

Attempting to cut down and even eradicate the unsuccessful and sadly, many successful suicide attempts from the bridge, former director of the Golden Gate Bridge Transit District, John Moylan campaigned to have some kind of anti-suicide measures put in place. In 2008, he suggested installing a net under the bridge that would catch anyone attempting to jump from it as well as putting up barriers to make it harder for people to climb and jump from the impressive structure. The barriers were eventually installed while talks on the netting continued.

But on the 5th of June, 2014, despite the anti-suicide barriers being put in place, someone still managed to climb out onto the bridge and jump to their death. That person was 27-year-old Sean Moylan from Novato, San Francisco. Sean was the grandson of John Moylan, the man who fought so hard to get the barriers put in place and prevent suicides, to begin with.

DRINK DRIVING COMEDIAN

Sam Kinison was a former preacher turned stand-up comedian and was very popular during the eighties. Famed for his raucous and loud performances while often telling offensive jokes during stand-up gigs, he also had a notable career in TV and movies. Kinison's humour was very near the knuckle and would often make fun of homosexuality, his ex-wives and more. Very un-PC stuff and not the kind of thing that would work with today's snowflake society. Kinison was known for his heavy drinking and would also use that as material for his jokes. One of his more notable jokes included references to drink-driving:

101

"We don't want to drink and drive... But there's no other way to get the fucking car back to the house! How are we supposed to get fucking home?"

His drinking and driving while drunk was no joke, he really did get behind the wheel of a car after heavy drinking sessions more than once. But on the 10th of April, 1992 he wasn't the drunk one, he was stone-cold sober. Driving his 1989 Pontiac Turbo Trans Am to a sold-out live gig in Laughlin, Nevada where he was set to perform. While driving down US Route 95, a pick-up truck crossed the centre line of the road and struck Sam Kinison's car head-on. Kinison suffered numerous severe injuries, including a dislocation in the cervical spine, a torn aorta, and torn blood vessels in his abdominal cavity, all of which caused his death within minutes of the collision. Also in the car was Malika Souiri, Kinison's new wife who he only married just six days before the accident, who survived with only a mild concussion.

Sam Kinison, 38 who was well known for his drinking and drink driving jokes, yet he was sober as a judge at the time of the accident, but the driver of the truck that caused the accident wasn't. He was 17-year-old Troy Pierson who pleaded guilty to one count of vehicular manslaughter and driving while intoxicated.

UNBELIEVABLE BUT TRUE DEATHS

Sometimes, you'll hear or read a story about death that is so ridiculous and outrageous that you'll believe it just can't be true. But as I said in the introduction to this book, each and every single one of the stories here are indeed true and thoroughly fact-checked, even the unbelievable ones in this chapter.

CACHI AND DOMINO THEORY

The domino theory is one that suggests that one single starting event could have a knock-on effect that goes on to affect another, then another then another and so on. Basically, like how an entire row of dominoes can be knocked over just from one single starting domino. Well Cachi the poodle from Buenos Aires, Argentina was the cause of such an effect in 1988.

It was the 24th of October of 1988 when Cachi the poodle fell to its death from a thirteenth-floor balcony in central Buenos Aires. But the dog wasn't the only fatality that day. It's not known exactly how or why Cachi fell and met its untimely death, but what is know was that the dog landed onto 75-year-old Marta Espina, who was out for a casual walk and both Cachi and Marta died instantly from the impact. If that was not bad enough, then Edith Sola, 46 who witnessed the accident stood in shock at what she had just seen... Unfortunately, she was standing in the road when she suddenly stopped in her tracks after seeing the falling killer canine and was hit by a passing bus, killing her instantly. By now, there was a crowd gathering and gawping at the carnage that had just occurred. One of the crowd was an elderly unidentified man who had suffered a heart attack and collapsed after seeing both the plummeting pooch kill Marta Espina and then the bus hit Edith Sola. The elderly man was rushed to hospital in an ambulance but died en route. Three humans and one dog dead all because Cachi the poodle fell from a balcony and no one knows why.

WARNING: FALLING BEEF

45-year-old Joao Maria de Souza was lying in bed asleep with his wife in Caratinga, Brazil in 2013. His small home backed onto a steep hill near some farmland. A little earlier and a cow had escaped the farm, which then found it's way onto the hill that shadowed Joao de Souza's house, a house that had a simple and very thin corrugated asbestos roof. The cow was happily grazing on the hill when it stepped onto that roof.

One and a half tons of uncooked steak fell through the weak roof of the house and onto the sleeping couple's bed. The cow just missed de Souza's wife, but he was not so lucky as the bovine landed on his side of the bed and Joao de Souza suffered a fractured left leg, but with no other obvious injuries, he seemed okay. Considering the fact he just had a whole cow fall around eight-foot and land on him, de Souza was relatively unhurt, except for the fractured leg that is. He was taken to hospital where his injuries were thought of as minor so was not seen as a priority. However, Joao Maria de Souza died the next day while waiting to be seen by a doctor as he had suffered internal bleeding which had not been previously diagnosed. Both the cow and de Souza's wife survived.

ONE LAST DRINK

To paraphrase the great philosopher and free thinker, Homer Simpson:

"Beer, the cause of, and solution to, all of life's problems."

Well on the 17th of October, 1814, beer was the cause of a huge problem, one which left several dead. The Horse Shoe Brewery used to stand on the junction of Tottenham Court Road and Oxford Street, London. The brewery became famed for its very popular porter, a very dark and malty beer.

It was around 4:30 PM when one of the workers of the brewery noticed that an iron band, which secured the huge vats used to brew the beer, had slipped down slightly. He told his supervisor who assured the worker there was no issue as the bands would occasionally slip during the brewing process anyway, so there was nothing to worry about. But around an hour later and the iron band completely came off the twenty-two-foot high wooden fermentation tank of beer and it suddenly exploded, the force of which also knocked off the stopcock from the equally huge vat sitting next to it, causing its contents to also burst free. Within seconds, around three hundred and twenty-three thousand gallons of The Horse Shoe Brewery's famous porter beer smashed through the wall of the brewery, sending bricks and debris into the roofs of nearby houses, causing mass amounts of destruction and devastation.

A fifteen-foot high wave of malty dark beer sweep through the streets of London and destroyed two houses. In one of the houses, 4-year-old Hannah Bamfield was enjoying dinner with her mother and a friend. The mother and friend were swept out into the street by the huge wave of beer, but sadly the toddler was killed. In the other house, there was a wake being held for a 2-year-old boy who had recently died. The mother of the boy, Anne Saville along with four other mourners, Elizabeth Smith, Catherine Butler, Mary Mulvey and her 3-year-old son, Thomas all died. 14-year-old Eleanor Cooper who was working at the Tavistock Arms pub was also killed as she was buried alive under the rubble from the brewery's wall when it exploded due to the flood of beer and another child, Sarah Bates was found dead from falling debris in another house near the brewery, she was only 3-years-old. Strangely enough, no one in the brewery itself was killed or even seriously injured.

There were reports that for several days after the beer explosion, that people were scooping up and drinking the gallons of porter beer that had swept into the streets and homes nearby. There were unconfirmed stories that several other people had died of alcohol poisoning from the free booze. After such a tragedy that left at least eight people, mainly women and children dead, The Horse Shoe Brewery even had the audacity to allow people to view the remains of the destroyed beer vats... And charge them money for the privilege too. The brewery eventually moved to new premises and stayed in business for a while until 1921 when it filed for bankruptcy.

GOING OUT LAUGHING

The Monty Python comedy troupe were famed for their nonsensical and punchline absent humour, they are responsible for some of the most famous comedy sketches ever to be seen. On the 5th of October, 1969, one of the Python's sketches called *The Funniest Joke in the World*, told the story of someone who wrote a joke so funny that could literally kill people by laughing themselves to death. In real life, the joke or the sketch itself didn't actually kill anyone, but another British comedy group's humour did. It was the 24th of March, 1975 when The Goodies (Tim Brooke-Taylor, Graeme Garden, and Bill Oddie) and their infamous *Kung-Fu Kapers* episode of their comedy show was first aired on the BBC. Sitting at home watching the show was 50-year-old Alex Mitchell, who was laughing at the show for around twenty-five minutes non-stop, which was pretty much the entire running time of the episode. His continual laughing put such a strain on his heart that he suffered a fatal heart attack and died right there on his settee. According to his then-wife, the scene that had Mitchell laughing the most was one that involved radio controlled black puddings attacking Bill Oddie near the end of the episode. Alex's widow later wrote a letter to The Goodies thanking them for making her late husband's final moments so enjoyable as he died laughing.

Strangely enough, many years later in 2012, Alex Mitchell's granddaughter, Lisa Corke, suffered, but survived a heart attack at the age of 23. She was later diagnosed with Long QT Syndrome, a condition that affects the repolarization of the heart after a heartbeat and can lead to sudden death. So, it is thought that Alex Mitchell himself possibly suffered from the same condition, which could be hereditary.

A VERY STICKY END

In the North End neighbourhood of Boston, Massachusetts, one of the most unbelievable disasters occurred, The Boston Molasses Disaster. The Purity Distilling Company was based at 529 Commercial Street near Keany Square, Boston. The company used to specialize in the production of ethanol through distillation, they stored molasses (a very thick, viscous and sticky black treacle) which was being brought in from the ships from the nearby docks. The molasses was then fermented to produce the ethanol the company was famed for.

On the 15th of January, 1919, a new shipment of molasses was put into the fifty-foot tall, ninety-foot diameter tanks that housed millions of gallons of the incredibly sticky and sweet substance. It's not known exactly how it happened, but it had been suggested that an increase in temperature was the main cause. The molasses would always be heated to thin down its viscosity which would help with transporting the extremely thick and sticky liquid. It was around 12:30 PM when the tank holding the molasses burst open and collapsed, freeing the many hundreds and hundreds of thousands of gallons of now warmed molasses. Witnesses at the time recall something that sounded like a bomb going off as the tank exploded, followed by a machine-gun-like sound as rivets from the tank shot out hitting everything in sight.

Molasses is about 40% thicker than water and that extra density helped the sticky liquid to gain some speed as a wave around twenty-five foot high moved at thirty-five miles per hour toward the neighbourhood. Buildings and homes were pulled from their foundations and crushed. The exact death toll is not known, but it has been estimated that around a hundred and fifty-odd people were injured and at least twenty one people were killed. Deaths included drowning as the thick and sticky molasses seeped into the victim's nose, ears and mouths and slowly suffocated them. Others were killed by the flying debris from the exploding steel tank and the devastation it caused to the surrounding buildings. So severe was the disaster that for decades later, locals said you could still smell the sweet odour of molasses on hot summer days. Pictures exist that you can easily find on the interwebs that recorded the incredible amount of damage caused by The Boston Molasses Disaster, multiple levelled buildings, destroyed elevated train tracks. It's actually quite amazing that only around twenty-one people were thought to have died when you see how much devastation was caused by what was basically black treacle.

OFF WITH HIS HEAD

Eastleigh, Hampshire and a local residential estate full of flats were earmarked to be demolished to make room for redevelopment. The flats had originally been built in the early sixties and were in desperate need of modernisation, all of the seventy-one flats had been emptied when it's residents accepted alternative accommodation. All except one that was still being lived in by 50-year-old David Phyall. According to reports at the time, Phyall had been 'irrationally opposed to moving' from the flat he had lived in for the past eight years. He refused a total of eleven offers of other and better accommodation from his housing association. No matter what he was offered, he just refused to move out of his out of date and soon to be demolished flat in Bodmin Road.

After a while, it all went silent when David Phyall stopped replying to letters and calls from the housing association. At first, it was thought he was just ignoring all contact as he refused to leave his flat, and it was believed he had become increasingly more stubborn. The whole thing was even taken to the courts to repossess the property by force. Police were called in to check on Phyall on the 5th of July, 2008, where they forced their way into his property. David Phyall's body was found lying under a snooker table in his flat. But he hadn't died from natural causes, no heart attack from the stress of being told he has to move. Next to his body was his own severed head and a bloody chainsaw. Phyall had managed to decapitate himself with the chainsaw and died instantly. David Phyall chose to die in his flat over leaving it for better accommodation. Swallowing a few pills probably would have done it, but cutting your own head off with a chainsaw makes a bigger statement I guess?

Simon Burge, deputy coroner recorded a suicide verdict and was quoted as saying:

"In the fifteen years I have been sitting as a deputy coroner, this is the most bizarre case I can recall."

NOT SO HAPPY DOUBLE CELEBRATION

Lottie Michelle Belk was celebrating both her 55th birthday and wedding anniversary on Virginia Beach, Virginia on the 8th of June, 2016. But the happy day was about to turn to horror. Belk was on the beach enjoying some family time taking in the surf and sun. But at around 5 PM, emergency services were called to attend to Lottie Belk who had just been involved in a freak accident. She was taken to a nearby hospital but died of her injuries shortly after.

But it was what killed her that makes this one unbelievable, it was an umbrella. Sitting in all that sun can be damaging to the skin and so keeping in the shade as much as possible is pretty important. Large beach umbrellas or parasols are often used to keep bathers safe from the sun's harmful rays. But, beach umbrellas are not like the ones you use when it's raining, they are much bigger, heavier and often feature a large wooden spike at the end used to stick them into the sand. As well as the sharp wooden spike, these hefty umbrellas are usually anchored to the ground too for extra safety. Alas, the umbrella that hit and killed Belk had not been correctly secured or anchored. When a twenty-five miles per hour wind kicked up, it took one of the beach umbrellas with it and what is normally used to protect people suddenly became a deadly weapon. Being forced along in a speedy wind, the spiky end of the umbrella slammed into Lottie Belk and implied her causing horrendous and fatal injures.

A VERY, VERY NON-VEGETARIAN DINNER

Armin Meiwes, 42 was a computer repair technician living in Rotenburg, Germany in 2001. Meiwes decided to look for a friend on the internet, which is nothing unusual, we all do it via various social media sites. But the place Armin Meiwes went looking for a friend wasn't Facebook, Instagram, Twitter or any of the sites used today. The place Meiwes used was very specialist because he wanted his friend to do something very specific. The website Meiwes used was called 'The Cannibal Café', a now-defunct forum for people with a cannibalism fetish. The post Armin Meiwes placed said that he was:

"Looking for a well-built 18 to 30-year-old to be slaughtered and then consumed."

Straight to the bizarre and macabre point, I guess and yet, weirdly enough, he got replies… Quite a lot of replies, in fact, all answering and accepting his request to be killed and eaten. Most of them backed out later except for one. Bernd Jürgen Armando Brandes, 43 who answered and agreed to be killed and eaten by Armin Meiwes in March, 2001.

The pair had arranged to meet at Meiwes' home on the 9th of March, 2001 and they even made a video of the entire event too. Now at this point, I just want to highlight the fact that Bernd Brandes was 100%, completely in agreement with everything and Armin Meiwes never once forced his willing participant to do anything against his will. It was all discussed and agreed to in advance. The two men had an agreement, a bloody and bizarre agreement I admit, and it followed through… Which makes the following even more unbelievable.

After being welcomed into Armin Meiwes' home, Bernd Brandes swallowed around twenty or so sleeping tablets, a bottle of cough syrup and then drank half a bottle of schnapps. After which Meiwes then cut off Brandes' penis, the original agreement was for Meiwes to bite it off, but that proved too difficult so it was cut off instead. The pair then attempted to eat the man-sausage raw, but couldn't as it was too tough. So Armin Meiwes cut it up into smaller pieces and pan-fried it with some salt, pepper, wine, garlic along with some of Bernd Brandes' own fat. The appendage was burnt while cooking and became inedible... If a pan-fried human penis can ever be edible that is, so Meiwes fed it to his dog instead. Just a quick reminder, this was all with complete agreement from Brandes and being recorded on video too.

After the unsuccessful attempt to cook the man-meat, Armin Meiwes ran Bernd Brandes a bath, who at this time was bleeding heavily. While Brandes bathed and waited for death, Meiwes casually read a Star Trek book, checking on his soon to be meal every few minutes. In the early hours of the following morning, Brandes climbed out of the bath and collapsed due to the loss of blood. He then drifted in and out of consciousness several times before falling unconscious one last time. He was still alive, barely. That was when Meiwes said a prayer and stabbed Brandes in the throat, killing him before hanging his body on a meat hook. Again, all agreed to and recorded on tape.

Over next the ten months, Armin Meiwes ate Bernd Brandes' body which he dismembered and placed in his freezer (less waste?). He ate around twenty kilos of Brandes' flesh cooked in olive oil and garlic which Meiwes said he enjoyed with South African red wine. He also said how he would always get out his best cutlery and decorated his dinner table with candles, adding on how the human flesh tasted a lot like pork. In December of 2002, Armin Meiwes was arrested when he placed another ad looking for another victim online. Police searched Meiwes' home and found what was left of Bernd Brandes in his freezer as well as a four-hour videotape of the event. But it gets even more unbelievable...

Cannibalism is considered perfectly legal in Germany, so in that regard, Armin Meiwes did nothing legally wrong. However, murder is very illegal. But, due to the fact that his victim was completely compliant and in full agreement with his own murder and they had all of it on video too (which was used in court as evidence), Meiwes could only be charged with manslaughter and was sentenced to just eight years in prison in January 2004. Oh yeah, there's more. A later retrial in April 2005 argued that he should've been charged with murder not manslaughter and his psychologist believed that Meiwes still posed a threat and had fantasised of killing and eating others. So Armin Meiwes was eventually convicted of murder on the 10th of May, 2006 and then sentenced to life in prison. One last tit-bit of unbelievability to end on, while in prison, Armin Meiwes became a vegetarian.

A SHEEPISH WAY TO GO

Ashes Quarry, Country Durham is a beautiful, picturesque and serene slice of the English countryside. Full of natural beauty, rolling green hills and sheep, lots and lots of woolly sheep. Experienced farmer's wife, Betty Stobbs, 67 was out doing her rounds of feeding the farm's sheep near Ashes Quarry. Riding around the stunning landscape on her quad bike with a bail of hay tied to the back, ready for the hungry ovines dinner time. She parked up the bike near the edge of the quarry, ready to feed her fluffy flock. Something Betty Stobbs had done dozens and dozens of times in the past. This time, however, would be her last.

As she got off her quad bike, around sixty or so sheep began to stampede toward her, hurrying toward the bail of hay. Several of the sheep jumped for the tasty dried grass and hit Stobbs, who stumbled back and fell more than a hundred foot into the quarry, the sheep also knocked her loyal sheepdog over the edge. But, Betty Stobbs, nor the dog died, they were injured lying on the jagged rocks of the quarry, but alive. Two of Stobbs' farming neighbours witnessed the accident and rushed over to help, but the rowdy sheep had not finished their meal. As they bustled around the quad bike carrying the hay, they slowly pushed the four hundred-odd kilogram bike closer and closer to the edge of the quarry. As the two good Samaritan neighbours ran to help, the quad bike kept inching toward its inevitable fall. The heavy bike eventually slipped over the edge and fell onto Betty Stobbs crushing and killing her. The sheepdog survived.

S. L. PERRIN

AT LEAST HE SMELT NICE

Jonathan Capewell, 16 was your average teenager from Oldham, Greater Manchester. Awkward around girls, had a bit of acne and suffered from body odour as the transition from boy to man began. We've all been there... Well, the males have anyway. It's a difficult time for any young man's life, it's confusing and strange. There's not much that can be done about the awkwardness with girls at that age, but the acne and smelly armpits can be treated. It was the latter of the two that Capewell became obsessed with.

He began to use an inordinate amount of deodorants. Often spraying his entire body multiple times a day. Jonathan Capewell's father said about his son's deodorant use that:

"Even when we were in a room downstairs we couldn't just smell it, we could taste it."

On the 29th of August, 1998, Capewell suffered a heart attack and collapsed in his bedroom, his 17-year-old sister found her brother lying on the floor and raised the alarm. But how/why did a perfectly healthy 16-year-old with no heart condition suffer a heart attack? It was his deodorant obsession. A post-mortem discovered that Jonathan Capewell had around 0.37 milligrams of butane per litre in his bloodstream and the same amount of propane too, a level of just 0.1 milligrams per litre can be fatal. The butane and propane entered and poisoned his bloodstream via his excessive use of deodorants. Jonathan Capewell was rushed to the hospital but was pronounced dead around ten minutes after arrival. Dozens of cans of deodorant were found in the teenager's bedroom, many of which were empty.

RAPUNZEL SYNDROME

16-year-old Jasmine Beever from Skegness, England suddenly became very ill while at college on the 7th of September, 2017. So, she left and returned home where she went straight to bed and soon after, Beever realised that her skin had turned red and blotchy. Beever collapsed and fell unconscious, an ambulance was called and she taken to hospital and successfully resuscitated... If only for fifteen minutes. Jasmine Beever died and at the time, no one knew how or why. She was perfectly healthy and had no previous medical issues.

It was later revealed that Jasmine Beever had an unusual eating disorder, one known as Trichotillomania or Rapunzel Syndrome. A disorder that meant the teenager liked to eat her own hair. Her family were fully aware of her bizarre eating habit but believed that nothing bad would ever come of it and that she would eventually outgrow the hair eating, how wrong they were. Over a prolonged period of time, the teenager ate enough of her own hair that it formed a hairball in her digestive tract. This hairball infected the thin membrane of her stomach lining which led to a deadly infection and she contracted peritonitis in her stomach, causing an ulcer to form. The ulcer eventually burst and this led to Jasmine Beever's internal organs shutting down and her death.

HIT AND RUN AND STUCK

In the early hours of the morning of the 26th of October, 2001, 25-year-old Chante Jawan Mallard was driving home from a party along Interstate 820, near Fort Worth, Texas. At the party, Mallard had been enjoying various substances, alcohol, marijuana and ecstasy coursed through her bloodstream as she drove home. The cocktail of partying into the early hours of the morning and the various substances in Mallard's system had impaired her judgement and slowed her reaction time, which is very dangerous for anyone driving. Chante Mallard rounded a curve to merge onto Route 287 and drove her car straight into a homeless man who had been walking along the dark highway, 37-year-old Gregory Biggs.

The force of the impact launched Gregory Biggs into the air, and he was catapulted onto the front of Chante Mallard's car. Biggs' head and upper body went crashing through the windscreen and landed on the passenger side of the inside of the car, while his legs remained trapped inside the windscreen on the outside of the car. He was quite literally stuck inside the windscreen. Mallard was so disoriented because of all of the drugs, that she didn't even realise that a human was stuck in her windscreen at first. When she eventually realise what had happened, she stopped the car, got out, and went around to try and pull Biggs free from the glass, but as soon as she touched his leg, she panicked.

In her drunk and drugged up state, Chante Mallard didn't know what to do next. So with Gregory Biggs still trapped in the windscreen, she drove to her house, pulled into the garage and closed the garage door behind her. Instead of calling emergency services, Mallard had sex with her boyfriend. Over the next few days, she would occasionally return to the garage to check on her hit and run victim until he eventually bled to death.

Chante Mallard then called on two friends to help move the body and dump it in a park, they even set fire to the front of the car in an attempt to remove any forensic evidence. Four months later and Mallard was at another party where he boasted about killing a white man with her car and begun cracking jokes about the whole incident. One of the people she was bragging to at the party informed the police and Mallard was soon arrested, put and trial and found guilty of murder in June 2003. She was given a fifty-year prison sentence for her crime. Medical experts at the trial said that if emergency services had been called, then Gregory Biggs would've easily survived the incident. Oh yeah, I almost forgot that Chante Jawan Mallard, the woman who failed to call emergency services to save the life of someone slowly bleeding to death worked as a nurse's aide.

THE DEATH OF MR. HANDS

People obtain nicknames for all sorts of reasons, often to express affection as a form of endearment and amusement. Kenneth Pinyan, 45 from Enumclaw, Washington earned himself the nickname of Mr Hands… But the reason why is pretty disturbing and unbelievable. How can I put this tastefully? Horses are traditionally measured for their height in hands, one had equates to four inches. Yup, that's how Kenneth got his nickname, but he didn't measure the height of horses, he errrr… Did something else.

It was the 2nd of July, 2005 at a farm in King County, Washington, a few miles from Enumclaw when Pinyan and two friends paid a visit to the farm, not for the first time and armed with a video camera. First, Pinyan filmed one of his friends being anally penetrated by a stallion. After which, they swapped and Kenneth 'Mr. Hands' Pinyan was the one being filmed while the stallion did what stallions are known for. During the sex, Pinyan complained of feeling great pain and soon passed out. He was taken to a hospital by one of his friends, who asked for help for Pinyan before quickly disappearing into the night.

Kenneth Pinyan was taken into the hospital but died in the emergency room shortly afterwards. The Medical Examiner's Office reported that Pinyan had died of acute peritonitis due to perforation of the colon and the death was ruled as accidental. If that was not unbelievable enough then how about this... Kenneth 'Mr. Hands Pinyan and his friends hadn't broken any laws as at the time, bestiality was actually legal in the fine state of Washington. It was only after the death of Kenneth Pinyan when Washington carried out the decision to make bestiality illegal.

NO LION OR WITCH

51-year-old Ronald McClagish was found dead in his bungalow in Murrow, Cambridgeshire in February 2004. His death was ruled as accidental despite its bizarre nature. McClagish's body was found trapped in a walk-in cupboard in his bedroom. It is thought that he had been cleaning out the cupboard when a heavy wardrobe fell against the cupboard door and trapped McClagish inside.

While trapped in the cupboard, Ronald McClagish grabbed a copper water pipe that ran through the enclosure and ripped it from the wall, which he used to try and smash his way through the door. Sadly, the cold water from the now broken water pipe began to gush all over his body. After his body was found and a post mortem was carried out, it was revealed that McClagish had died from bronchitis that was either caused by the cold water or that he had been already suffering from an infection and the water from the pipe made it much worse. Police were called to the bungalow after neighbours complained about hearing banging sounds as McClagish tried to free himself. When the police discovered Ronald McClagish trapped in the cupboard, the water was still free-flowing over his body.

McClagish's family were convinced that something more sinister had happened. They didn't believe that the wardrobe fell on its own and suggested that someone broke in and trapped Ronald McClagish in the cupboard. But after an investigation, there were no signs of forced entry or a struggle of any kind except for McClagish's vain attempt to escape. A coroner recorded an open verdict into the death, meaning they found the death suspicious, but no proof to record a specific verdict.

TAKING THE BLUE PILL

Sergey Tuganov, a 28-year-old mechanic from Russia made a bet that he could sexually satisfy two women in a twelve-hour threesome in 2009. The money on the table was the equivalent of around £3,000, so this was a bet worth taking on. Tuganov had a plan that would help him maintain his performance for the half a day long sexcapade, he had vodka... And Viagra. He swigged at the vodka and downed the entire bottle of the little blue pills... The entire bottle. You know what, he won the bet too. With little help from the popular erectile dysfunction pills. Just for the record, side effects of Viagra can include acid indigestion, diarrhoea, skin flushing, headache and nasal congestion. Even more severe but very, very rare effects include blindness, heart attack, stroke, high blood pressure, cardiovascular symptoms, and even sudden death... And that's from just one pill. Sergey swallowed the whole bottle, which contained around thirty or so pills.

He may have won the bet and presumably had a fantastic twelve hours of sex, but he never got the chance to enjoy his winnings. Soon after his sexual feat, Sergey Tuganov dropped dead of a heart attack.

"We called emergency services but it was too late, there was nothing they could do."

Claimed one of the female participants who I assume was very tired and extremely sore.

LONG TIME DEAD DEATHS

When we die, however we die, we hope that to save our dignity that we will be found and taken care of with respect and as soon as possible. Sadly, some people die and they are not found for weeks, months, years or even decades at a time, slowly left to rot and decay.

THE LOST BOYS

On the 8th of August, 1973, Dean Arnold Corll was shot and killed by Elmer Wayne Henley in Houston, Texas. But don't feel too bad for Corll though, as he was a notorious serial killer who abducted, raped, tortured, and murdered at least twenty seven teenage boys between 1970 and 1973, in what became known as the Houston Mass Murders. Don't praise Henley for his killing of a paedophile serial killer either because… Well, it's a long and complicated story that you can look into yourself.

Anyway, after Dean Corll was shot and killed, Elmer Henley led police to a metal storage shed, which Corll had been renting. Inside were the bodies of some of his victims. It took a whole week for the police to conduct a thorough and detailed search of the shed and its surrounding area as they recorded every last detail of the many bodies found inside and buried in the ground nearby. A total of twenty-seven bodies were found, some as young as 13-years-old at the time of their deaths. All of them had been sexually assaulted, sodomized and tortured. Some had their genitals chewed, others had been completely removed. Nylon ropes still wrapped around their necks, some with bullet holes in their heads. Many of the bodies were in various states of decomposition and found wrapped in clear plastic sheets. Despite finding the remains of twenty-seven young boys, Elmer Henley claimed that twenty-nine or more boys had been kidnapped and killed, but the other bodies were never discovered. In fact, a total of forty-two young boys had gone missing in Houston in the early seventies and many believe that some of them, if not all, were victims of Dean Corll.

All of the bodies that were found were those of teenagers that had gone missing up to three years previously. Many families who had lost their children in the early seventies held out hope over several years that one day, they would be reunited with their sons, but that was a hope destroyed by the uncovering of the bodies. The gruesome discovery of, what was at the time the worst case of serial murder in the United States, was a big news story and also when many parents first learned that their long lost children would not be coming home. Many of the bodies were assumed to have been there for around three years before being discovered.

MUMMY AND DAUGHTER

Unemployed 50-year-old Caroline Jessett cared for her 78-year-old mother, Pauline for several years after she had become disabled due to a horse-riding accident. They lived together in their home in Littlemore, Oxford. Police were called to their home in 2013 when neighbours reported that they hadn't seen or heard from neither mother nor daughter for several months and that the house had fallen into disrepair.

Environmental health officers entered the home first to find a very dilapidated house. There were piles of unopened letters dating back at least seven months, the foliage had grown through holes in the brickwork, furniture was covered in thick dust and cobwebs, the entire property had basically been left to rot. Police carefully made their way to one of the house's bedrooms to find the body of Caroline Jessett lying next to a desk, an electric fan sitting on the desk was still running. On the 21st of November, 2013 the house was declared structurally unsound and had to be made safe before police could re-enter the property and piece together exactly what had happened. After searching the house once it was made safe, they found another body. That of the mother, Pauline who had been placed in a bath and covered with blankets and sheets. Both bodies had been lying dead for so long that they were described as being mummified and a formal identification could only be made via forensic techniques.

It was worked out that Pauline must've died first, possibly sometime in early to mid-2012. After the death of her mother, Caroline Jessett found it hard to cope with her loss and also died in early 2013. Post-mortem examinations carried out on both bodies were unable to determine a precise cause of death. Coroner, Darren Salter recorded a verdict of natural causes for Caroline Jessett, suggesting she died from a brain tumour. But an open verdict for her mother, Pauline was ruled, as he said it was impossible to determine her cause of death.

BODY IN THE WALL

A contractor was working on a house in Poughkeepsie, New York on the 28th of June 2013. The house belonged to James L. Nichols who had died a few months earlier in December 2012. As he carried out his work of examining and clearing up the home, the contractor discovered a fake wall and behind that wall was a large plastic rubbish bin. The bin contained a human skeleton wrapped in a plastic sheet.

Back on the 26th of December, 1985, James Nichols reported that his wife, Jo-Ann had gone missing. James told police that his 55-year-old spouse had left for a hair appointment at a local beauty parlour, only she never returned home. James also told police how his wife had become severely depressed after the death of their son by drowning in 1982. He suggested to the police that there is a possibility that Jo-Ann left home to commit suicide. Of course, that's not what actually happened.

The body found hidden behind the fake wall was that of Jo-Ann Nichols, she was later identified by dental records. Her body had decomposed to a skeleton with her hands still tied with rope. A large area of the right side of the skull was also missing where it had been hit repeatedly. Her cause of death was put down to blunt force trauma to the head. It seems that James killed his wife and hid her behind the fake wall, where her remains would not be found for another twenty-seven years. As James Nichols died before his wife's skeleton was discovered, he was never punished for his crime and it's not known exactly why he murdered his spouse and never will be.

WIVES CAN DO IT TOO...

Coming off the back of the previous story comes a very similar one but with the roles reversed. John and Leigh Ann Sabine were a loving husband and wife living in New Zealand in the 1960s. Over the years, they had a total of six children, all of which were abandoned in a state-run nursery in Auckland. The couple then moved to Australia where

Leigh attempted to become a nightclub singer, which proved to be a failure when her singing career never took off. After a few years, they moved back to New Zealand and in the mid-eighties, they even attempted to get back in touch with their children… That didn't work out. So John and Leigh Sabine moved to England, and this is when things turned to murder.

They travelled around England for a few years living in various places around the country, before settling down in a small former coal-mining village, Beddau, South Wales in 1997. That was also the last time that John Sabine was ever seen alive. In December of 2015, Leigh Sabine died of cancer aged 74.

It had been eighteen years since John Sabine was last seen alive in 1997 to when Leigh Sabine died in 2015. John's skeletal remains were discovered wrapped in more than forty layers of plastic wrapping, roofing felt and shopping bags. The body was left in the loft of the house and found days after Leigh had died, by a family member cleaning out Leigh's home. John's remains were still dressed in his Marks & Spencer pyjamas when uncovered. Strangely enough, the dead body parcel had previously been found at Leigh's home, but she told friends who'd ask about it that it was just a medical skeleton that she had bought for a joke to play on her husband. A post-mortem carried out revealed that the cause of death was blunt force trauma to the head and a heavy stone ornamental frog was the murder weapon, which was found hidden in plain sight in the garden. Before she died, Leigh Sabine boasted to friends that she could be famous after she dies and how people would talk about her… Well, I don't know about fame, but she made it into this book at least.

HANGING AROUND THE APARTMENT

Thomas Ngin lived in an apartment in Bussy-Saint-Georges, Paris. He lived alone, didn't really talk to his neighbours and kept himself to himself. When his mailbox began to fill up with letters, Ngin's neighbours got into the habit of emptying it and returning the post to the post office believing he had left the county and returned to Cambodia where he was originally from, sometime in 2005. In 2013, the apartment was seized by Thomas Ngin's bank after the bills mounted up and put on the market when it became clear that after eight years of absence, he would not be coming back.

In October of 2015, someone finally bought the apartment from an auction and prepared to move in. First things first, they needed to clear the apartment out of all of Ngin's belongings. A locksmith was called to gain access to the new tenant's abode. As the new owner entered, there was something behind the door making it difficult to get in, after a few hard pushes, the door opened enough for the apartment's new owner to get inside. What was blocking the front door was the rotten and hanging body of Thomas Ngin.

An investigation revealed that Thomas Ngin had killed himself eight years previously in 2005, after losing his job as a security guard. At the time, he had cut all ties with family and friends, he even had two brothers and two sisters who lived not too far away in France, but none of them had any contact with him for years. Thomas Ngin would've turned 50-years-old just a few days after his body was found.

NOT SO HAPPY CHRISTMAS

In January 2006, officials from a north London housing association had to repossess a bedsit in Wood Green due to increasing and mounting debts. Officials forced entrance to the bedsit and the first thing they noticed was a pile of unopened post at the door, some dated as far back as 2003. They could hear a noise, it was a television still on and tuned to BBC 1. They called out to check if anyone was home but they got no reply. The officials then entered the main living area and that was when a waft of decay hit their nostrils. A small pile of unopened Christmas gifts and cards were neatly stacked near the sofa, but it what was on the sofa which was the biggest shock.

The rotten and mostly skeletal remains of an adult woman were lying on the sofa. The body was so badly decomposed that she could only eventually be identified by dental records and by using an old holiday photograph of her smiling. She was 38-year-old Joyce Carol Vincent. Investigating police searched the bedsit and found food in the fridge with use-by dates for 2003. Given the dates on the food, the post and the unopened Christmas gifts, police believed Joyce Vincent must have died in December 2003, three years before her body was found in 2006. Pathologist Dr Simon Poole was unable to establish a definite cause of death due to the fact the body was largely skeletal but he believed it was down to natural causes.

LONG LOST SKIER

Sonja Barnes' 24-year-old brother, Gregory Barnes was an avid and very active outdoors-man type. He mysteriously disappeared in 1980 while skiing in the Italian and Swiss Alps with friends. In September of 2015, Sonja received a rather unexpected phone call from Italian police informing her that her brother's body had finally been found, thirty-five years after he had gone missing.

Gregory's corpse was discovered due to a hotter than normal summer which had caused a glacial melt, revealing his long lost body. Gregory's passport was found on him which made the formal identification easy. When police spoke to people he was with at the time, it was concluded that Gregory Barnes went on a skiing trip to northern Italy. There he met up with other like-minded outdoor enthusiasts and a small group of them set out to climb Bernina peak in the Eastern Alps to do a spot of skiing. The group were making their way up the mountain range together when Gregory said that he was having trouble with his ski bindings, so he returned to the hut they were staying in at base camp to fix the problem. Once sorted, he then tried to catch up with the rest of the group, but lost his way and fell into a deep crevasse and died. The alarm that Gregory had gone missing was raised at the time, but the search parties found nothing. It took thirty-five years and a bit of sunshine before Gregory Barnes' body could be found and recovered.

THIRTY-FIVE YEARS? TRY OVER THREE HUNDRED

Bishop Peder Winstrup was born on the 30th of April, 1605 and died on the 28th of December, 1679. He was Bishop of Lund in Scania, now modern-day Sweden. After his death, he was placed in a coffin and buried in a crypt in Lund cathedral, Sweden. Nothing unusual so far and living for seventy-odd years before dying was a damn good life in the 1600s, plus the fact it's expected to find a body in a coffin means this entry is pretty bog-standard so far.

But, it was June 2015 when something surprising was revealed. Using modern technology, scientists scanned Bishop Winstrup's coffin, so they could carry out research on his life and social conditions. The scan not only revealed one of the most well-preserved bodies of the 17th century, Winstrup's clothing still intact and his face recognisable from paintings of the time and so on. But, it also showed other human remains in the coffin with him, those that belonged to a baby, estimated to have been around 5 to 6-months-old. The body of the baby had been deliberately hidden under Bishop Winstrup's feet.

But why was he buried with a baby and why try to hide it? A question we will never know the answer to, there has been some speculation. It has been suggested that the baby may have been the illegitimate child of the respected Bishop and that it was buried with him to hide his shame. But, as he was 74-years-old when he died and the baby was estimated to have been only a few months old, maybe that's not quite right? It's not known if the baby was alive or dead when it was buried with the Bishop, nothing is known about the baby's connection to him either. Given that this all happened around three-hundred and thirty-six years before the scan in 2015, it's very doubtful the truth will ever be known about the mysterious, three-century-old buried baby.

A VERY SLOW SUICIDE?

On the 3rd of February, 2013, 54-year-old Carla Ruth Reyes went missing. She was last seen leaving her home in Yucca Valley, California by neighbours. Reyes left her belongings behind including her phone, so there was no way to contact her. The next time she was seen was when a group of hikers discovered her car parked near Joshua Tree National Park on the 27th of October, 2015 with Carla Reyes' dead body inside. Over two years after she was last seen alive by anyone.

Her family confirmed that Reyes suffered from alcoholism and depression, and they believe her death was suicide. An autopsy confirmed Carla Reyes' identity, but could not determine her cause of death, though no foul play was suspected and there were no signs of a struggle or anything to suggest that anything underhanded had happened to her. It seems that Reyes could not handle her depression and just wanted to go away. She left no note, no explanation, she just left. But, there is a little mystery. Her car was found in an area only used for four-wheel-drive vehicles, which Carla Reyes didn't have. When found, her car was stuck in the sand of a very remote area of the desert. So perhaps she just got lost while out driving and became stranded? Maybe it never was suicide to begin with?

AND ANOTHER ONE (AGAIN)...

Pia Farrenkopf, 49 was a bit of a loner, even her family wouldn't hear much from her, sometimes for years at a time. She loved to travel and would often go to places like Amsterdam, Austria, Ireland, Las Vegas and Italy without ever telling anyone. Her family would receive the odd postcard or phone call from one of the corners of the world, and that would be the first time they knew that Farrenkopf had gone away. Even her neighbours knew she would disappear for long periods at a time and they just got into a habit of mowing her lawn for her when the grass overgrew. So, when no one had heard from her for a few years, nothing seemed out of the ordinary, her family thought she had just gone travelling again and would hear from her whenever Pia Farrenkopf could be bothered to make contact. Her neighbours continued to mow her lawn as they had always done, everything seemed to be perfectly normal.

Pia Farrenkopf had a good chunk of money in the bank from her very lucrative job as a contractor for Chrysler Financial, so her bills would get paid regularly and on time, via automated billing. It was in 2014 when Farrenkopf's home was foreclosed on, after her bank balance had been rung dry and the bills were no longer being paid. Cleaners were called into Farrenkopf's home in Pontiac, Michigan to clear out any mess and empty the house of its contents. That was when Pia Farrenkopf's body was discovered. It was in the back seat of her Jeep still parked in the garage. The body was described as being heavily mummified. Using bank statements to create a timeline of when Farrenkopf was last active, it was estimated that she must've died sometime in early 2009, a little over five years before the bank foreclosed on her home and her body was found.

An investigation into her death showed no wounds, no forced entry to the property, no reason to suggest any kind of foul play or self-harm had occurred whatsoever. There was no note left either. It couldn't have been

124

carbon monoxide poisoning as her Jeep still had a full tank of fuel, which after five years, would not be the case as the tank would've emptied long before then if it had been left running. Pia Farrenkopf's death is a mystery and the fact she was found in the back of the Jeep and not the front adds another layer. Farrenkopf's family do not believe it was suicide as they say that would've been very out of character. But, with no signs of foul play, suicide seems the only logical cause. The fact it had been over five years from when Pia Farrenkopf died to when she was found, made making a formal reason for her death pretty much impossible to find. The cause and manner of death were both ruled as undetermined. It seems like she sat in the back of her Jeep and just stayed there until she died.

FISHERMAN'S DISCOVERY

A local fisherman was out on Hillsdale Lake in Paola, Kansas in 2015 looking to score a good catch. Wanting to get the upper hand on the aquatic animals, he used an underwater sonar scanner to seek out the gill bearers, only he discovered something bigger than a fish. Around a hundred or so feet from a boat ramp in the lake, the fisherman's sonar scanner picked up a large object that looked like a vehicle. The fisherman called the local police who turned up and pulled the object from the lake via a tow chain.

The fisherman was right, it was indeed a vehicle. A 1981 Chevrolet Citation in fact, and sitting in the driver's seat was a body. After an investigation, the police learned that the car was registered to Fremont O'Berg, a 57-year-old who was reported as missing in 1992, twenty-three years before the car was found in 2015. A formal identification couldn't be made due to the decomposition of the body, nor could a reason be found for why O'Berg and his car ended up at the bottom of Hillsdale Lake. But given the fact Fremont O'Berg had gone missing in that area over twenty years ago and that the car found was registered to him, it was pretty clear he was the body sitting in the driving seat.

When O'Berg was first reported as missing in 1992, a search of the area including Hillsdale Lake was carried out, but nothing was ever found. Whether it was an accident and Fremont O'Berg left the road unintentionally or drove into the lake on purpose will never be known.

His family said that he suffered from heart disease and acute bronchitis and police believe this could've been a factor in his death.

VERY LATE FOR WORK

Larry Ely Murillo-Moncada, 25 was last seen on the 28th of November, 2009. He used to work at the No Frills brand of supermarkets in his home city of Council Bluffs, Iowa. His mother reportedly said that Murillo-Moncada used to suffer from hallucinations and how he often used to hear voices. Larry Ely Murillo-Moncada was put on antidepressants, but the medication didn't appear to help much or at all. On the evening of the last time he was seen, he rushed out of the house barefoot in the freezing snow and vanished into the night. A search was organised but it seemed that Murillo-Moncada had just disappeared without a trace.

The supermarket where Larry Ely Murillo-Moncada had worked closed down in 2016, seven years after he had gone missing. In 2019, contractors were called into the supermarket to clear the place out. They started by removing all the shelving before being tasked to take all the refrigeration units from the store. As the moved one of the twelve-foot tall fridges, a badly decomposed body was found behind it. The body was that of Larry Ely Murillo-Moncada who had gone missing ten years earlier. The gap behind the fridge was only around eighteen inches, yet somehow, Murillo-Moncada had managed to squeeze himself into it. Bearing in mind that the supermarket had been open for seven years from when he had disappeared to when it closed, so customers still used the fridge he was trapped behind and yet none of the workers found the dead body either. Goes to show how rarely they must have been cleaned. The supermarket where Murillo-Moncada worked and was found was less than half a mile away from his home too.

He was still wearing the same clothes and still barefoot from when he was last seen, which suggests that he must have left home and gone straight to his workplace that night. Yet, nobody saw him arrive at work, nobody thought to search the store either when he went missing. Exactly how or why Larry Ely Murillo-Moncada ended up stuck behind a fridge is not known. His death was ruled as accidental.

BOOK OF DEATHS

TEA AND TV

In Zagreb, Croatia, 1966, Hedviga Golik sat down with a cup of tea to watch some television. Forty-two years later in 2008 and Golik's mummified corpse was found, still sitting in her chair with that cup of tea undistributed next to her on a nearby table. A police spokesman said:

> "When officers went there, they said it was like stepping into a place frozen in time. The cup she had been drinking tea from was still on a table next to the chair she had been sitting in and the house was full of things no one had seen for decades. Nothing had been disturbed for decades, even though there were more than a few cobwebs in there."

For forty-two years Golik had been left dead in her apartment… But here's the unbelievable bit. She was actually reported as missing at the time back in 1966, and the windows of her home had been left open too. But, no one thought to check the place Hedviga Golik lived in when she was reported as missing, and yet no one wondered why the windows were open all year round for over four decades either? Police, neighbours, no one thought to just see if there was any chance she could still be in her home while conducting a search for her?

Just as with other stories in this chapter of bodies being found several decades after they had died, due to the decomposition of Hedviga Golik's corpse, there was no way to determine an exact cause or even an accurate date of when she died. She was born in 1924 and last seen alive in 1966, so she would've been around 42-years-old at the time, the same amount of years from when she was last seen alive to when she was found in 2008.

NATURE LOVER

Joshua Vernon Maddux, 18 from Woodland Park, Colorado loved nature and would often go out for long walks in and around the stunning, one million acre Pike National Forest. It was on the 8th of May, 2008 when Maddux said goodbye to his sister before heading out on one of his much-loved nature walks as he would often do. However this time, he never returned home. A search was arranged for the missing teenager that lasted for seven years, it included family, friends and locals, all spending as much time as they could out looking for Joshua Maddux. Yet nothing was ever found, not a single clue.

Due to his age of 18, people assumed that Maddux must've just run away in a fit of teenage angst. But he had a happy home life and a loving family, he had no reason to run away. It was in 2015, seven years since Joshua Maddux had disappeared when a builder began demolishing his wooden cabin. The cabin hadn't been used for around ten years or so and had fallen into a state of disrepair. There was a smell of decay in the air of the cabin, but that was put down to the fact it had been disused for over a decade. As the demolition of the wood cabin continued, Joshua Maddux's decomposed, skeletal remains were eventually discovered and found in a very unusual place too.

He was found stuck in the stone chimney of the cabin, there was no evidence of foul play, no signs of trauma. It was assumed that perhaps Joshua Maddux had climbed onto the roof and had tried to climb down the chimney to gain access to the cabin and got stuck. Al Born, the coroner who undertook the autopsy said:

> "The hard tissue showed no signs of trauma. There were no broken bones, no knife marks. There were no bullet holes. There is so far no answers to a number of things. It is very confusing."

Joshua Maddux's death was put down to either dehydration or hypothermia and ruled as an accident.

FINAL DESTINATION DEATHS

Final Destination is a horror film from 2000 that tells the story of a bunch of teens who manage to escape death, after being taken off a plane that explodes during take-off, when one of them has a premonition. Though they cheated death, the Grim Reaper still seeks them out and they begin to die off one by one in various ways. It's a work of complete fiction of course... But life has been known to imitate art.

A STING IN THE TAIL

21-year-old Austin McGeough was a soldier stationed at Fort Campbell located on the Tennessee-Kentucky border in the US. It was during the early hours of the morning in October 2016 when McGeough was attending a party. Witnesses at the time said that the had been combining copious amounts of alcohol with the painkiller Percocet, which he had been given following surgery to remove his wisdom teeth the day before. The mixture of booze and drugs had an effect on McGeough, and so he went for a walk from the party to help clear his head. Later, he tried to return to the party only to find that the place had been locked up. Austin McGeough wanted back in, he found a broken window covered with cardboard awaiting repair. Seeing this as an opportunity to rejoin the merriment and drink more booze, he punched out the cardboard with the idea to unlock the back door. Only there were a couple of problems.

The first issue, the building he was trying to gain access to was not the same location as the party he had left earlier. The alcohol and painkiller cocktail had left McGeough very disorientated, and the building he was trying to break into was in fact a nursery that had closed for the day, not the scene of the party. The second issue was, that behind the cardboard covering the broken window was a freshly build wasp nest. Now, the thing to remember here is that wasps are not like bees who die after one sting. Wasps can sting multiple times. Combine that with a nest full of wasps and that is hundreds and thousands of painful stings, and that many stings can kill someone. So, as Austin McGeough punched his hand through the cardboard covered broken window, his fist smashed into the wasp nest, thousands and thousands of angry wasps came looking for whatever just destroyed their home. McGeough ran for it and somehow managed to lose his angry and very possible killer chasers as he sprinted away through the night.

Soon realising that he was lost, McGeough headed to the nearby Highway 41A in Pleasant View, Tennessee and tried to hitch a ride back to civilization. He ran out into the busy road and was hit by a car being driven by Emily Prisock. Austin McGeough hit the front of the car and his head smashed into the windscreen, before falling into the road. Prisock stopped to see what she had hit, or more accurately, what had hit her. As she tried to warn other motorists that someone was lying in the road, two other cars ran over Austin McGeough, killing him, without stopping.

Edit: Since originally writing this part of the book, further developments have been made. Originally, it was reported that Austin McGeough was on his phone talking to emergency services and he had told them that he was being chased by wasps. But now the wasp chasing has been brought into question. At around 3:27 AM, McGeough did call 911 to say he was being chased, but he never said by who or what.

Cheatham County Sheriff's Investigator Jeff Landis has said that:

"McGeough did not appear to be in fear of his life, but sounded agitated. The 911 audios revealed McGeough's speech was slurred. Close to the end of the audios, it appears McGeough realizes he is speaking to authorities. McGeough stops mid-sentence and refuses any assistance. McGeough cancels his request for help."

Austin McGeough last spoke to 911 at 3:45 AM, he was struck by the car being driven by Emily Prisock at around 3:58 AM.

LIFE SAVERS?

The emergency services are here for our own safety and security. They do an amazing job and save hundreds, thousands, millions of lives all over the world every year. But sometimes, things can go very wrong. It was the 6th of July, 2006 when Asiana Airlines flight 214, a Boeing 777 crash-landed at San Francisco International Airport. The plane was trying to land, but it came up short when approaching the runway and crashed into a seawall at the edge of the landing strip. Amazingly, only two people died in the crash, with most surviving, but the crash did leave a hundred and eighty-one people injured. One survivor was 16-year-old Ye Meng Yuan, she was thrown from the back of the plane as it crashed when it had its tail ripped off, as it attempted to land. Yuan landed just a few meters from the flaming wreckage. Emergency services rushed to the scene to put out the fires and help all of the injured.

As ambulances and fire trucks arrived to assist, Ye Meng Yuan was curled up in the foetal position scared, hurt and in need of serious medical help. Sadly, the driver of a fire truck did not see the teenager and ran her over. If that was not bad enough, then a different fire truck turned up eleven minutes later and ran over her once more as it moved to a different location on the runway to help put out the blaze.

San Mateo County Coroner Robert Foucrault concluded that Ye Meng Yuan was still alive when she was hit by the two fire trucks, stating that there was sever internal haemorrhaging which indicated her heart was still beating at the time as she was hit by the first truck. He also said:

"We did our examination and we determined that the young lady was alive when she was struck by the fire trucks."

It had been suggested that if Ye Meng Yuan had not been hit by the fire trucks, then she could've survived the plane crash with treatment. Instead, she added to the small death toll to make it three fatalities.

THE DARK KNIGHT SHOOTING

Jessica Redfield was an aspiring writer and journalist. She had just landed a job as an intern at a Denver radio station as a sports broadcaster/reporter. Redfield loved her sports, especially hockey and she would often write about her passion on her blog. On a sunny Saturday afternoon in June 2012, Jessica Redfield was in the food court of the busy Eaton Centre shopping mall in Toronto, Canada. After eating a burger, Redfield told friends at the time how she had a feeling of unease and discomfort, so went out to get some fresh air. Only a few moments later, Christopher Husbands entered that same busy food court and randomly fired fourteen shots into the crowd. Two people were killed and several others injured from both the bullets and the stampeding crowd running to safety. If Jessica Redfield had not gone out to grab some air at that time, she could've added to the death count. After surviving the shooting, Redfield posted an entry on her blog which read:

> "I can't get this odd feeling out of my chest. This empty, almost sickening feeling won't go away. It's hard for me to wrap my mind around how a weird feeling saved me from being in the middle of a deadly shooting.

> I was shown how fragile life was, I saw the terror on bystanders' faces. I saw the victims of a senseless crime. I saw lives change. I was reminded that we don't know when or where our time on Earth will end. When or where we will breathe our last breath. I say all the time that every moment we have to live our life is a blessing. So often I have found myself taking it for granted.

> Every hug from a family member. Every laugh we share with friends. Even the times of solitude are all blessings. Every second of every day is a gift. After Saturday evening, I know I truly understand how blessed I am for each second I am given."

A very clearly emotionally upset Jessica Redfield was lucky and very thankful that she lived through that shooting. It was just a few weeks later on the 20th of July, 2012 when Redfield attended a midnight screening of the then-latest Batman film, *The Dark Knight* in a Century 16 movie theatre in Aurora, Colorado. Shortly after the film began, James Holmes entered the screening and set off tear-gas grenades before firing at the audience with multiple firearms. Up to that point, it was the deadliest mass shooting in Colorado, since the Columbine High School massacre in 1999. *The Dark Knight* shooting left seventy people injured and twelve deaths. One of those deaths was Jessica Redfield who, a little over a month earlier managed to survive the Eaton Centre shopping mall shooting.

As of writing, Jessica Redfield's Twitter account is still active. Her last couple of Tweets on the 20th of July, 2012 mention how happy she was at going to the screening of *The Dark Knight*.

BOOK OF DEATHS

SURVIVING 9/11

It really goes without saying that the cowardly terrorist attacks that changed the world on that infamous day were horrific. With billions of dollars in property damage, over six thousand people injured and sadly, two-thousand-nine-hundred and seventy-seven deaths. One of the blackest days in recent history, or even ever. Amazingly, some people who were working in the Twin Towers at the time survived. One such survivor was Hilda Yolanda Mayol, 25, who worked at a restaurant at the World Trade Center when the attacks happened. The restaurant that Mayol worked at was on the ground floor so she and others were able to escape before the towers came down. But escaping one tragedy led to another soon afterwards.

It was just two months later after 9/11 and almost to the day, when Mayol was on American Airlines Flight 587 on the 12th of November, 2001. The plane was flying from Queens, New York to the Dominican Republic where Hilda Mayol was planning on spending time with her mother. The plane crashed into a neighbourhood of Queens shortly after take-off, it was one of the worst aviation disasters in American history. Amazingly, only five bystanders were killed on the ground, but all two hundred and sixty people on board the plane perished, including Hilda Mayol, who had managed to live through the 9/11 terrorist attacks. Due to the fact that the plane crashed, and only a couple of months after 9/11 too, the initial concern was that the plane had been brought down via another terrorist attack. However, An investigation showed the plane actually crashed due to a fault with the vertical stabilizer, which had broken off shortly after take-off.

NOT SO LUCKY ESCAPE

It was the 13th of December, 1977 when the Purple Aces basketball team from the University of Evansville, Indiana had a big game. The team boarded a twin-engine small plane headed for Murfreesboro, Tennessee to take on the Middle Tennessee State University team. The plane was only ninety seconds into its flight after take-off when it suddenly crashed in a nearby field. No one on the ground was hurt, but everyone on board the flight perished. A total of twenty-five people died instantly in the crash, another three died at the scene after the crash, while a further victim died later in hospital. Leaving twenty-nine people dead that day, including flight crew members, representatives of the University of Evansville and the whole of the Purple Aces basketball team... All except for one.

18-year-old David Furr was also a member of the Purple Aces. However, he had to sit the big game out due to suffering an ankle injury just a few days prior. Furr managed to escape the terrible fate that befell his fellow teammates. Yet, only two weeks later and David Furr himself would also die in a tragic accident. Out for a drive with his younger brother Byron, 16. A drunk driver came speeding around a blind bend and careened head-on into Furr's car. The drunk driver escaped with minor injuries but both David Furr and his younger brother were killed instantly in the collision.

PARTY PLANNING

Kiss nightclub in Santa Maria, South Brazil housed a huge party for the students of the Federal University of Santa Maria, on the 26th of January, 2013. The party had been party organised by Jessica de Lima Rohl who also helped to sell tickets to her fellow students. Also attending the party were the popular Brazilian band, Gurizada Fandangueira. The band were known for their use of fireworks during their shows. During their set at the party, one of the band's members lit a pyrotechnic device which launched into the air and exploded. Unfortunately, the explosion ignited some highly flammable acoustic foam in the ceiling and a fire quickly spread during the early hours of the following morning on the 27th of January.

The entire nightclub was soon engulfed as the young students ran for safety. Due to the lack of fire exits and the fact the club exceeded the maximum capacity by hundreds, a total of two-hundred and forty-two people died with more than six hundred and thirty others injured. Only eight of the deaths were due to injures suffered by burns from the flames, all the others were a result of smoke inhalation and being crushed by the panicking students trying to flee the fire from the club's only exit. It was one of the worst fire disasters in Brazilian history, and yet one of its main organisers, Jessica de Lima Rohl was not there that fateful night. She fully intended to attend the party and was getting herself ready too, that was when she received a strange phone call from her boyfriend, Adriano Stefanel, 20 who pleaded to de Lima Rohl not to go. He couldn't explain why, but he just had a feeling that she shouldn't go to the party... His feeling was right too. Jessica de Lima Rohl agreed to stay at home while many of her and Adriano Stefanel's friends died. After the fire, Jessica de Lima Rohl saw her boyfriend as a guardian angel and would follow his advice without question. Santa Maria's city government established thirty days of official mourning for those lost in the fire.

The following day, after the tragic incident and Adriano Stefanel posted the following message on social media:

"After what happened in Santa Maria, so many people I knew lost their lives. To those who are still here, thank God and pray for those people who have gone, and for their families that they will have the strength to get over such a great loss."

Yet only ten days later, there would be another tragic loss. Just over a week after the fire that claimed the lives of over two hundred and forty young students, many of which were friends of both de Lima Rohl and Stefanel, the couple were driving back to Santa Maria from the town of Toledo, when their car was hit head-on by a truck, both were killed, Jessica de Lima Rohl died instantly in the crash, while Adriano Stefanel succumbed to his injures later in hospital.

MISSED THE PLANE

Johanna Ganthaler from Italy was taking a well deserved holiday in Brazil with her husband, Kurt. The couple were due to take the Air France Flight 447 from Rio De Janeiro to Paris on the 31st of May, 2009. After which, they then planned to drive from Paris to their home in Italy. However, they were running late on the day of the flight and missed the plane by just a few minutes. Now stranded in Brazil, they found a hotel for the night before securing another flight, this time to Germany for the next day. The flight they missed, Air France Flight 447, came crashing down into the Atlantic Ocean around four hours after take-off killing all two hundred and twenty-eight people on board.

The following day, Johanna Ganthaler and her husband boarded their flight to Germany which landed safety in Munich, after they managed to luckily avoid the previous fateful plane crash. The couple hired a car and set out to drive from Germany back to their home in the Bolzano-Bozen province, Italy. As they drove through Kufstein, Austria, they lost control of the car which swerved into the oncoming lane and crashed into a truck. Johanna Ganthaler was killed instantly but her husband, Kurt managed to survive the crash after suffering serious injuries and recovering in hospital.

YOUTUBE DEATHS

The video sharing site YouTube has some very contradictory rules. Swearing in videos is frowned upon and can lead to demonetisation and even being outright banned, sex and nudity are also not allowed. But blood and gore is seemingly okay. Even more so, actual real-life deaths can also be viewed on YouTube, and this chapter looks at some of those deaths that you can freely watch as of writing. Quick disclaimer: I've watched these videos to write this book, but I wouldn't recommend that you do as some are very graphic and highly disturbing.

BUDD DWYER

Serving between 1981 to 1987, Budd Dwyer was the 30th State Treasurer of the Commonwealth of Pennsylvania. He was a loving family man, married with two kids. In the early eighties, it was revealed that public employees of the Commonwealth of Pennsylvania had overpaid millions of dollars in Federal Insurance Contributions taxes. Money that had to be refunded. Several accounting firms competed for the multimillion-dollar contract to determine the compensation to each of the employees. A contract to investigate and return all the overpaid taxes was eventually awarded to the firm Computer Technology Associates (CTA). Later, the Governor of Pennsylvania received an anonymous memo alleging that bribes had been exchanged for CTA to get the $4.6 million contract. Long story short, Budd Dwyer had been mentioned by name as one of the people who had received around $300,000 in bribes.

On the 18th of December, 1986 after further investigation and a very long trial, Dwyer was found guilty of eleven counts of conspiracy, mail fraud, perjury and interstate transportation in aid of racketeering. He faced a prison sentence of up to fifty-five years and a $305,000 fine. Yet, through the entire investigation and trial, Budd Dwyer maintained his innocence, claiming that he never accepted any bribes at all.

On the 22nd of January, 1987 the day before he was due to be sentenced for his crime, Dwyer arranged a press conference which was filmed and shown live on TV. At the conference, Dwyer began to read out from a twenty-one page prepared speech that he had written. The speech was very long and lasted around half an hour or so, as he read from it, some of the press began to pack away their cameras out of sheer boredom. Budd Dwyer noticed this and said:

"Those of you who are putting your cameras away, I think you ought to stay because we're not, we're not finished yet."

The speech continued, and as Dwyer got to the final page, he called out people who he said had betrayed him as he still protested his innocence. Budd Dwyer even name-checked the judge who handed him the fifty-five-year prison sentence by saying:

"Judge Muir is also noted for his medieval sentences. I face a maximum sentence of fifty-five years in prison and a $305,000 fine for being innocent. Judge Muir has already told the press that he felt 'invigorated' when we were found guilty and that he plans to imprison me as a 'deterrent' to other public officials. But it wouldn't be a deterrent because every public official who knows me knows that I am innocent. It wouldn't be legitimate punishment because I've done nothing wrong. Since I'm a victim of political persecution, my prison would simply be an American Gulag."

Dwyer's speech continued, but he never finished it. As he was on the final page of his lengthy speech, but before the end, he called on three of his staff and gave each of them a letter. One letter was for the then Pennsylvania Governor Bob Casey. The second was addressed to deputy press secretary Gregory Penny and it contained Budd Dwyer's organ donor card. The third and final letter was for Dwyer's wife and children. After handing out the letters, Budd Dwyer reached into his briefcase and removed a manila envelope, inside the envelope was a Smith & Wesson Model 27 .357 Magnum revolver. The crowded room of gathered press and government officials began to panic as Dwyer held the gun in his hand, worrying he was going to open fire on the crowd, but he didn't. Instead, Dwyer tried to calm and reason with the panicking crowd. He even gave them the chance to leave the room when he said:

"Please, please leave the room if this will… if this will affect you."

Some of the people left to get help, others stayed and tried to plead with Dwyer to drop the gun. He began to back up against a wall while pointing the gun in the air and asking for people to stay calm, never once raising his voice, never once coming across as a threat. Budd Dwyer then placed the barrel of the gun into his mouth and squeezed the trigger.

The news crews at the time caught the public suicide on film and it's very easy to find on YouTube. Budd Dwyer slumped backwards against the wall as blood poured from the exit wound and his nose. Dwyer died instantly from the gunshot and was pronounced dead at 11:31 AM on the 22nd of January, 1987. However, there is a little sting at the end of this one. After his death, it was proven that Bud Dwyer was innocent of all charges. He never accepted any bribes and that he had been set up by others. The 2010 feature-length documentary film, *Honest Man: The Life of R. Budd Dwyer* details the evidence that Dwyer was innocent. It is believed the reason that Budd Dwyer killed himself, despite his innocence, was so that his family would benefit from a government payout after his death. The final part of the speech that Dwyer prepared, but never read, was found with the rest of his notes after he killed himself and it read:

"I've repeatedly said that I'm not going to resign as State Treasurer. After many hours of thought and meditation I've made a decision that should not be an example to anyone because it is unique to my situation. Last May I told you that after the trial, I would give you the story of the decade. To those of you who are shallow, the events of this morning will be that story. But to those of you with depth and concern the real story will be what I hope and pray results from this morning in the coming months and years, the development of a true justice system here in the United States. I am going to die in office in an effort to see if the shameful facts, spread out in all their shame, will not burn through our civic shamelessness and set fire to American pride. Please tell my story on every radio and television station and in every newspaper and magazine in the US. Please leave immediately if you have a weak stomach or mind since I don't want to cause physical or mental distress. Joanne, Rob, Dee Dee - I love you! Thank you for making my life so happy. Goodbye to you all on the count of three. Please make sure that the sacrifice of my life is not in vain."

S. L. PERRIN

ALISON PARKER AND ADAM WARD

Journalism and reporting can be a highly dangerous job, some journalists go to literal war zones to report on the news. But then, there is the softer side of reporting, the nice little interviews with everyday, local folk that offer zero danger or peril. Yet, this story covers the deaths of two people reporting on the latter, far away from any notable threat. Alison Parker, 24 was a news reporter who, along with photojournalist Adam Ward, 27 were both working for CBS affiliate WDBJ in Roanoke, Virginia. The pair had been sent out to conduct a live interview with Vicki Gardner, who was the executive director of the local chamber of commerce near Smith Mountain Lake in Moneta, Virginia. This was as far removed from a dangerous situation as you could get, picturesque Mountain Lake is hardly Iraq. The interview was broadcast live on WDBJ's breakfast TV show *Mornin'* on the 26th of August, 2015.

The interview began in the early hours of the morning at 6:46 AM, as it was being broadcast on live TV, eight loud bangs were heard before the camera fell to the ground. Abruptly cutting back to the studio where presenter, Kimberly McBroom is caught unaware and unsure of what just happened. When interviewed about the incident later, McBroom said:

"I thought maybe a car backfired. I thought maybe there were shots in the background. The county is kind of rural."

But sadly, a car backfire was not the source of the noise, it was a Glock 19 9mm pistol held and fired by Vester Lee Flanagan, 41 (AKA Bryce Williams).

Vester Flanagan used to be a reporter for WDBJ, the same company both Alison Parker and Adam Ward worked for. Flanagan was sacked in 2013, he later tried to sue the station claiming discrimination, but the case was eventually dismissed. Both reporters, Parker and Ward were shot along with their interviewee, Vicki Gardner. Gardner was wounded, but she survived the shooting after surgery. Sadly, Alison Parker and Adam Ward were not so lucky, both were shot in the head and pronounced dead at the scene.

140

BOOK OF DEATHS

Now, there are actually two videos of the murders. One was being recorded by Adam Ward, as the interview took place and was broadcast live on TV. The other was recorded by the killer, Vester Flanagan. Using a body-cam, he recorded the double murder. After the shooting and fleeing the scene, Flanagan made a post on Twitter saying:

"I filmed the shooting see Facebook."

He wasn't lying either. Vester Flanagan had uploaded the video to Facebook for people to see and it showed Flanagan casually walking to where the interview was talking pace, just a few feet away as to not be seen. He then waits for the interview to start, ensuring they were broadcasting live, Flanagan makes the very short walk toward his intended targets before raising the gun firing multiple shots at point-blank range. Both his Twitter and Facebook accounts were shut down just a few hours after the shootings, but they were up long enough for the video to be shared and downloaded. Put out on the internet, along with the one broadcast live filmed by Adam Ward.

After murdering Alison Parker and Adam Ward, Vester Flanagan made a run for it and escaped in a rented car. Police did catch up with him later (after he uploaded the murder video to Facebook) but just followed, trying to avoid a high-speed pursuit, as he was known to be armed and dangerous. When more units joined, the decision to try to stop him was made. A state trooper attempted to pull Flanagan over at around 11:30 AM, just a few hours after the double murder, but he sped away and a chase began. However, shortly after and Flanagan's car just ran off the road on its own. When police got to his car, they found Vester Lee Flanagan in the driver seat with a gunshot wound to his head. He was taken to a hospital, but was pronounced dead two hours later.

ROGER WILLIAMSON

Driving cars at high speed around race tracks can be a very entertaining but dangerous sport, the pinnacle of which is Formula One. Over the years, several drivers have lost their lives doing what they love, but perhaps none of them was quite as horrific as the day British driver Roger Williamson died. Williamson was making his début appearance in Formula One racing in 1973. He had previously raced in Formula Three and became a two time World Champion too, he had more than earned his stripes to drive in Formula One.

His first race in the greatest of all motorsports was at the British Grand Prix on the 14th of July, 1973. The race became infamous among Formula One fans for its massive first lap crash that caused a total of eleven cars to retire from the race, one of them being Roger Williamson in his March-Ford. Failing to impress in his first-ever Formula One race (through no fault of his own), Williamson was looking for a better result in the next race held at Dutch Grand Prix at Zandvoort Circuit... Sadly, to not only be his second Formula One race, but also his last.

It was on the eighth lap of the race when Roger Williamson suffered a tyre failure. His car flipped upside down and dragged across the circuit for several feet. His March-Ford caught fire and while Williamson was, rather miraculously, not actually harmed by the impact of the incident, the blaze was a very different story. The flames quickly spread and soon engulfed the entire car which continued to burn while Williamson was trapped underneath the overturned car. A close personal friend and fellow driver, David Purley, was just behind Roger Williamson in the race and saw the incident first hand. He quickly stopped his car and rushed to try and save his friend. Purley first tried to push the car back the right way up, but the weight and ever-increasing flames made this impossible. He then ran across the still active race track to get a fire extinguisher and hurried back to his burning friend. A few race marshals joined the chaos and tried to help, but the heat from the now out of control fire was way too intense to get close enough to the burning car.

David Purley tried to put the fire out with the extinguisher to no avail, as the helpless marshals could do nothing but look on. At the time, fire-proof clothing has not yet been introduced for track-side marshals. Purley doesn't give up and continually asks for help to save his friend, but receives none, nothing can be done. The video shows a very angry and dejected David Purley left with no choice other than to stand back and watch as his friend is trapped under the blazing car. It took just over eight minutes for a fire engine to arrive on the scene and finally put the fire out, by which time, Roger Williamson had died from asphyxiation along with severe burns from the fire, and it was all shown on live TV.

BOOK OF DEATHS

When talking about the incident later, David Purley said how he could hear Roger Williamson's screams as he tried to save his friend's life. Purley was later awarded the George Medal for the bravery, for trying to save Williamson. That one death changed motorsport from that day forward as it was made mandatory for track-side marshals to wear fire-proof clothing so they could help if anything like that happened again... And it did. The fire-proof clothing rule would save the life of legendary driver Niki Lauda who in 1977, was involved in a very similar accident that left him trapped in a burning car at the German Grand Prix.

SKNYLIV AIR SHOW

When something is widely known as 'the deadliest air show accident in aviation history', you know it has to be a bad one. It was the 27th of July, 2002 at the Sknyliv airfield near Lviv, Ukraine when this disaster occurred. More than ten-thousand people attended the show to commemorate the sixtieth anniversary of the Ukrainian Air Force's 14th Air Corps. It was meant to be a happy day of celebration and admiration for the troops, but it ended in scores of deaths and hundreds of injures instead.

A Soviet Sukhoi Su-27 fighter jet that was being flown by pilot Volodymyr Toponar and co-piloted by Yuriy Yegorov. Two very experienced men, who showed off various dangerous but impressive manoeuvres in the sky to the cheering of several-thousands of people on the ground. The jet engaged a downward rolling manoeuvre which took it to a very low altitude. It rolled upright but was still descending when the left-wing of the aircraft hit the ground. Within less than a second of the impact, the pilots ejected and escaped with only minor injuries, the same could not be said about the many spectators.

The jet then flattened out and crashed into a crowd of spectators before skidding along the ground and hitting a stationary aircraft, which caused the crashing jet to cartwheel and explode into even more spectators. There was nothing they could do as the fireball and fighter jet careened towards them. Mass panic ensued as people ran in all directions, but those that were caught amid the carnage died. A total of five-hundred and forty-three people were injured that day with seventy-seven spectators losing their lives, including twenty-eight children. It was a

143

scene of utter destruction and death. As with all of the stories in this chapter, various videos of the crash filmed by the spectators at the time can be found on YouTube.

On the 24th of June, 2005 both pilot Volodymyr Toponar and co-pilot Yuriy Yegorov were sentenced to serve fourteen and eight years in prison respectively, by a military court. The two pilots were found guilty of failing to follow orders, negligence, and violating flight rules. Three other officials of the event were also sentenced to prison time, between four to six years each.

1955 LE MANS

From the worst air show accident to the worst motorsport one. The 24 hour Le Mans race held in the town of Le Mans, France is the world's oldest and still active endurance race, it began in 1923 and is still held to this day. Drivers and car manufacturers gather from around the world each year to take part in this gargantuan race. The Circuit de la Sarthe where the race is held is a mix of closed public roads and specially built race track. Drivers race for a total of 24 hours in 'shifts' and the winner is not necessarily the first person to cross the finish line, but more a case of the driver/team that covers the greatest distance in the 24-hour-period.

The 24 hour Le Mans race has seen its fair share of accidents over the years, but none so deadly as the tragedy that occurred on the 11th of June, 1955. Not only the worst crash in the entire history of the Le Mans race, but the most horrific and fatal crash in motorsport ever.

The crash started when Mike Hawthorn pulled his Jaguar over for a pit-stop. Races today have dedicated pits lanes where cars slow down to enter. Back then it was just a case of pulling over at the side of the road with zero safety in place. So as Hawthorn pulled over for his pit-stop, he cut in front of the Austin-Healey behind him that was being driven by Lance Macklin. Macklin had to quickly swerve out of the way of the rapidly slowing Jaguar cutting across to the pits. As Lance Macklin tried to avoid crashing into Mike Hawthorn's car, he swerved and cut in front of another driver, Pierre Levegh in a Mercedes-Benz. Unable to stop or move in time, Levegh's car slammed into the back of Macklin's Austin-Healey and the Mercedes-Benz literally drove over the car that just cut in front of it, which resulted in Pierre Levegh and the Mercedes-Benz launching into the air.

Modern motorsports have high metal fences and protective barriers to keep spectators safe in case of a cash, they didn't have those in 1955 and the crowds could sit, quite literately, track-side with little to zero protection at all. So as Pierre Levegh's speeding Mercedes-Benz launched into the air, it went flying directly toward the watching crowd at around a hundred and fifty miles per hour. The car began to fall apart as it hit the spectators making at least two major impacts. One was with a concrete stairwell which was disintegrated via the impact. Debris from the car began to fly and cause numerous injuries and deaths. Pierre Levegh himself was thrown free from the crash as cars then didn't have seatbelts, and he landed on the track where he suffered a fatal head injury... But that was just the start. The debris from the crashing car spread far and wide including the bonnet of the car, which acted like a guillotine and decapitated numerous spectators, as it scythed through the air at great speed. The heavy engine careened through the crowd and rolled for around a hundred meters or so, crushing even more people to death. Some people climbed on scaffolding to get a better view of the race, but even they were not safe from the carnage and found themselves in the path of the deadly flying debris causing even more deaths. Driver, Duncan Hamilton saw the crash from the pits and recalled the accident when interviewed in 1964:

"The scene on the other side of the road was indescribable. The dead and dying were everywhere; the cries of pain, anguish, and despair screamed catastrophe. I stood as if in a dream, too horrified to even think."

But even after all of that death and destruction, it was still not over. The rear of the car landed on an embankment near the spectators and went up in flames when its fuel tank exploded. The destroyed Mercedes-Benz was made with a then-new Elektron magnesium-alloy body, which due to its high magnesium content burst into white uncontrollable flames. The explosion showered the already horrified and panicking crowd with white-hot magnesium embers and car debris, causing even more injuries and deaths. To make things even worse, rescue workers were not familiar with magnesium-based fires and threw water on to the flames, which only made things far, far worse as the fire intensified and burned for several hours before finally burning itself out.

So horrific was the accident that a fully accurate death toll has never been made. There were so many numerous body parts, crushed, decapitated and burned corpses (including children) that making a fully accurate count of those lost was impossible. But it is estimated that around eighty people lost their lives that day with a further one hundred and seventy-odd injured, though witnesses at the time say the death count was much higher than estimated. To this day, the 1955 Le Mans crash is still the most catastrophic and deadliest in motorsport history. So terrible was the accident that a temporary ban on all motorsports was put in place over Europe while track safety was improved. The crash and its video makes from some truly disturbing viewing as the dead, blood-covered bodies of men, women and children are pulled out from the carnage and laid on the track.

RICARDO LÓPEZ

Most fans of celebrities are relatively normal, some can get a bit obsessed with their idols, try to imitate them or even attempt to look like them. Others can take things too far and allow that obsession to take over. Ricardo López was a fan who took his love for his idol way, way too far.

López lived in the city of Hollywood, Florida where he worked in pest control, he was as normal as the next man... Or so it seemed. Ricardo López became a fan of Icelandic musician Björk in 1993 and soon became fixated with her. López began to write fan letters which started out perfectly normal, just praising the singer and her talent, a fan wanting to share his appreciation towards his idol, as a great many fans have done before him. But as time went on, the letters became more and more unhinged as López grew more disconnected from reality. He also began writing a diary where he detailed how he wanted to be a part of Björk's world and how he could be a positive element of her life. Though he professed to love the singer, he also wrote in his diary how he never felt anything sexual for her, in one entry he wrote:

"I couldn't have sex with Björk because I love her."

His dairy grew and grew to over eight hundred pages, each page detailed how much he loved Björk and wanted to be with her. López even wrote how he wanted to create a time machine to go back to when Björk was a little girl and become friends with her then, so they could grow up together. His fantasies became ever increasingly more bizarre.

In 1996, Ricardo López was in his apartment and read an article in a magazine about Björk being in a relationship with DJ and music producer, Goldie. The news upset López and pushed him over the edge. He began to think up ways of how to punish Björk for 'betraying' him and their 'love'. López quit writing the diary and then began recording his feelings and thoughts on video instead. Several hours of footage was recorded and has now been uploaded to the internet, so you can see how the simple man descended into madness for yourself. Ricardo López's obsession and love for Björk quickly turned to hatred and he began to plan ways to kill the singer. In one of his videos he says:

"I'm just going to have to kill her. I'm going to send a package. I'm going to be sending her to hell."

López first comes up with the idea of making a bomb with hypodermic needles filled with HIV-contaminated blood, which he would send to Björk via her record label, with the intent to infect the singer with the tainted blood. Realising making such a bomb would be far too difficult (it's not as if you can buy HIV blood in the shops is it?), he settled on creating a letter bomb containing sulphuric acid that would be hidden in a hollowed-out book, again to be sent to Björk via her record label... So that's exactly what he did.

It was on the 12th of September, 1996 when Ricardo López went to the post office and sent his home-made acid bomb with the intent of killing Björk. It was also the day he made his final video, which he titled *Last Day - Ricardo López*. After posting the bomb, López returned to his apartment and filmed his final moments alive. He stripped naked and shaved off his hair before painting his head red and green. Ricardo López put on some of Björk's music and danced around the room, as the song *I Remember You* finishes, he shouts:

"This is for you!"

López then places the barrel of a .38 calibre revolver into his mouth and pulls the trigger, killing himself instantly.

A few days later and a neighbour noticed a foul smell and blood seeping out from under Ricardo López's apartment door. The police were alerted and they found his body along with the handwritten diary and the numerous videos he had recorded. It was only when the police investigated the videotapes and got to the final one when they learned of the bomb that had been sent to Björk, who was living in London at the time. Scotland Yard got involved as the race to stop the bomb reaching the singer began. Fortunately, the package had not yet been delivered and was stopped at customs before it could make it to it's intended target. Ricardo López hoped the home-made bomb would kill Björk and that his suicide would unite them in heaven.

A documentary called *The Video Diary of Ricardo López* was released in 2000 and it contains edited footage of López's twenty-two hours long video diary and his disturbing obsession over Björk. There are various versions of the video diary that can easily be found on YouTube, most of them do not include the actual suicide... But if you really look hard enough, I know of at least one of them does.

TORTURES DEATHS

Going in our sleep is everyone's preferred way to die. Painless and peaceful. But throughout history, we humans have devised and carried out some of the most brutal and horrific deaths via torture that is far from painless or peaceful. This chapter looks at some of the most disturbing and disgusting ways humans have dispatched of their fellow man (or woman) over the years.

SCAPHISM

This particular torture method at first sounds quite nice as the intended victim is fed milk and honey. Of course, it wouldn't be in this book if it was that pleasant. Scaphism, also known as 'the boats' was dreamt up by the ancient Persians sometime in the 5th century. Devised to inflict as much pain and discomfort as possible, all while trying to keep the victim alive for as long as they could. Scaphism was kept for the most despicable crimes such as murder or treason.

The victim would be tied into a specially built boat facing upwards towards the hot sun, then another boat would be placed on top, trapping the person inside, but in a way that left their head, hands and feet exposed. The boats would also be placed in an area such as swampland to ensure there was wildlife nearby. The victim would then be force-fed milk and honey, if they refused to swallow, their torturer would prick their eyes with a sharp implement until they complied. As the victim would often refuse to swallow, a lot of the milk and honey mixture would end up spilling over their face, covering their eyes and neck, etc. The sweet smell of the liquid attracted the attention of the nearby wildlife of the swamp, normally insects at first, who would begin to eat the sticky milk and honey... And the victim's exposed head and face.

But if creepy-crawlies slowing eating your flesh was not enough, the sickly milk and honey concoction would also cause diarrhoea and seeing as they were tied into a boat-trap, there was only one place the diarrhoea could go. The victim slowly became weak and dehydrated as the boat filled with foul-smelling human waste, which attracted more and more wildlife. But the dehydration and diarrhoea aren't what would kill the person trapped in the boats, because each day they would be force-fed more and more milk and honey, which kept them alive for days or even weeks.

As the diarrhoea continued to fill the boat, maggots would eventually breed, this is where it got really nasty. The maggots and ever-increasing population of insects and sometimes larger wildlife such as rats would eventually find their way inside the victim, either via the mouth or even by eating their way inside. Once in the body, the numerous creatures would then eat the victim from the inside out. This is what would ultimately kill them. After the person trapped inside the boat was dead, the two boats would be separated finally revealing what (little) was left of their body. Perhaps the most famous victim of scaphism was a Persian soldier by the name of Mithridates, who was given this terrible death after he killed Cyrus the Younger during the Battle of Cunaxa in 401 BC. The following description is taken from the text *Plutarch's, Life of Artaxerxes*:

"The king decreed that Mithridates should be put to death in boats; which execution is after the following manner: Taking two boats framed exactly to fit and answer each other, they lay down in one of them the malefactor that suffers, upon his back; then, covering it with the other, and so setting them together that the head, hands, and feet of him are left outside, and the rest of his body lies shut up within, they offer him food, and if he refuse to eat it, they force him to do it by pricking his eyes; then, after he has eaten, they drench him with a mixture of milk and honey, pouring it not only into his mouth, but all over his face. They then keep his face continually turned towards the sun; and it becomes completely covered up and hidden by the multitude of flies that settle on it. And as within the boats he does what those that eat and drink must needs do, creeping things and vermin spring out of the corruption and rottenness of the excrement, and these entering into the bowels of him, his body is consumed. When the man is manifestly dead, the uppermost boat being taken off, they find his flesh devoured, and swarms of such noisome creatures preying upon and, as it were, growing to his inwards. In this way Mithridates, after suffering for seventeen days, at last expired."

BOOK OF DEATHS

IMPALEMENT

I always thought the idea of impaling a person was done so with a sharp and pointed spike that would kill the victim by puncturing their innards, making the death quick but as painful as possible. However while researching this, I discovered it was actually the opposite.

This rather brutal torture method was commonly used by the Hittites, Assyrians, Egyptians and even the Persians. There are various versions of impalement, but this particular one covered here originated sometime in the 18th century BC. Impalement was sometimes used to display the already dead bodies of enemies and criminals as a warning to others. But the most common and cruellest method was much more disturbing. The pole used would be blunt and not sharp as I thought. This was so the pole could go all the way through the body and not do any serious harm to the internal organs, as they were gently pushed aside, instead of being seriously damaged. The way for the pole to enter would either be via the vagina or anus, but seeing as one of those 'entrances' is limited to half of the populous, the anal route was used more commonly.

Anyway, a (usually) wooden and sturdy pole which was thinned at one end, but still blunt would be greased up and stuck in the ground. The poles would differ in length depending on the hight of the victim for reasons that will soon become clear. But usually, the pole would be just slightly higher than the person being impaled as if they were standing on tip-toes. The intended victim was then raised over the top of the pole and gently lowered onto it, with some guidance. If the pole was too wide and didn't fit the entrance, then a knife would be used to cut from the anus to the genitals to accommodate and ensure a tight fit. The victim was then lowered onto the pole until they could stand on their tip-toes.

So the pole is now inserted and the victim is impaled and still alive, but forced to stand on their toes... Hence the importance of the length of the pole. The victim would then have to stand there for as long as possible. They would slowly weaken and slip further and further down the pole, going from tip-toes to feet fully on the ground. As the days tick by, the victim continues to grow weak and slide down the pole. The grease and blood that would now be dripping down the pole would also attract insects that would begin to feed at the entrance point, adding to the pain and torture. As the pole is blunt and not sharp, it would force it's way up through the body as the victim slowly slipped down, it didn't damage any internal organs and just pushed them aside, making the pain last even longer while keeping the victim alive for as long as possible as they bled out. How long the victim lasted before dying would vary from person to person. Some people would last only minutes before dying, while others could last several days before slowly bleeding to death with a large wooden pole inserted into their rectum. This version of impalement was eventually seen as unnecessarily cruel (no shit!) and would be replaced with crucifixion. And about that…

CRUCIFIXION

Exactly how people died from crucifixion is debated even today. Some say that death came about due to hypovolemic shock, basically, a loss of fluids that prevents the heart from pumping sufficient amounts of blood to your body. Others have argued that death came about from crucifixion when other wounds on the body would send blood clots to the heart. Doctors have even suggested that people died via a 'voluntary surrender of life'… Whatever that is? While some have said that the death was a slow one due to exposure or thirst after being on the cross for days. However the cause of death came about, crucifixion was pretty horrific.

Well, I guess the most famous crucifixion is that of Jesus. The image of the crucifix is known worldwide that depicts Jesus nailed to the cross. Yet, this most famous method is perhaps the least known used at the time. People would be attached to the cross in various ways. Being crucified upside down with their hands tied together is one variation. Crucified the right way up was the most common, but instead of being nailed, the victims were usually just tied in place. The reason nailing the hands was not used all that often was because of the fact that the person's entire weight of their body would be held in place just via a couple of nails in the hand. That weight would cause the nail to tear through the flesh or they could easily pull their hands over the nail and the person being crucified could (very painfully) break free. Some people were nailed through the wrists which would prove much harder to break free from. And that's just the upper body, the lower didn't get much more comfort either.

Some victims would also have their feet nailed to the cross. Others had their legs broken. Either way, the pain would've been excruciating. The thing about the lower body being rendered useless is that (as mentioned), the upper body would have to do all the work. Whether you were nailed or tied to the cross, your shoulders would eventually separate and come out of the sockets. Sometimes, a footrest of sorts would be nailed in place to allow the victim to support their lower body. This at first sounds quite welcoming, but if you think about it, that just means you'd be hanging there for much, much longer and your inevitable death would be prolonged even further.

Crucifixion came in numerous methods, the famous one is the use of a cross, but some methods ever used the cross at all. Sometimes the victim would just be tied/nailed to a wooden beam that would be held in place above the ground via rope. One method just involved the victim's hands and arms being tied over their heads and hung in place. This would put pressure on the chest and the arms would come out of the sockets making it increasingly more difficult to breathe. Unable to get enough oxygen, the victim slowly suffocates. Try it yourself, put your arms above your head and stretch as hard as you can, then and try to breathe at the same time. You'll notice you can inhale with relative ease, but feel it much more difficult to exhale again and begin to feel increasing pressure on your chest the more you breathe.

It has been recorded that some people managed to survive being crucified and if they did, they were allowed to continue living. There is even a devotional practice of self-crucifixion where people volunteer to be non-lethally crucified for a limited time on Good Friday in the Philippines that still goes on today.

FLAYING

Perhaps one of the more grotesque torture methods that ever existed. It's not known exactly when the idea to remove the skin from a fellow human came about, but most experts and records suggest it started sometime around 911 BC. Flaying also seems to have been used by pretty much every ancient civilization at one point or another from The Aztecs to Medieval Europeans. The only major difference being that the Aztecs usually waited until their flaying victims were dead. Usually, while others much preferred to skin theirs alive ensuring the victim felt as much pain as possible before death.

Different cultures had slightly different techniques and methods of removing the skin from humans, but the end result was always the same. The aim was to remove the skin from the body, which would be secured in place by ropes or straps around the wrists and ankles, as slowly and as painfully as possible, all while keeping the victim alive. The Assyrian Empire liked to begin their removal of the skin by making cuts into the victim's buttocks or upper thighs and begin there. The Europeans tended to start at the feet and work their way up. The Chinese liked to start with the face and work down. Others would begin by cutting the flesh from the chest and work like removing a jacket.

Once the skin was removed and peeled away from the muscle tissue, still with the victim very much alive, the body was understandably very vulnerable. Death could occur from various factors. If the initial shock and pain of having your skin removed while you were still alive didn't kill you, then blood loss or hypothermia would. But even if you managed to survive all of that, then the inevitable infections from not having any skin would definitely finish you off after a few days... And yes, some victims of being flayed alive lasted for several days with no skin before dying. The skin was often used as macabre displays or used as a warning and a deterrent to enemies.

There have been several depictions of flaying through numerous paintings over the years such as *The Judgement of Cambyses* by Gerard David, *Apollo Flaying Marsyas* by Jan Janssens and *Flaying of Marsyas* by Titian to name a few. Worth looking at if you fancy some particularly bloody and gruesome art.

RAT TORTURE

Sometimes, the name of the method pretty much tells you everything you need to know doesn't it? Whatever you think rat torture is... That's pretty much exactly what it is. It's one of the simplest and yet, also one of the most terrifying methods of torture to ever exist. Rats have always had a bad reputation as dirty, disease-ridden rodents that'll eat anything... Including human flesh.

BOOK OF DEATHS

There are actually various different techniques of rat torture that have been used through the years and though they all differ, the two connecting elements are rats and a human body. One version was known as the 'half cage'. This would involve the victim lying on their back, usually tied to a table/rack. A small metal cage would be placed onto their abdomen and in that cage was a rat. The cage would then be slowly heated up and the rat would do it's best to try to escape the heat to no avail. The rodent's only option would be to use its sharp claws and teeth to rip its way through the victim's flesh. The rat would gnaw it's way into the victim's bowels as it tried to escape.

The 'rectoscope' was another version. This one was a favourite of the South American's, particularly the Argentinian military as recent as the 1970s. A telescopic tube would be inserted into the intended victim via the rectum or vagina. Then a rat would be placed at the entrance of the tube, which would then be blocked off to prevent it from escaping, leaving only one way to go... Inside. The rat would then scurry around, clawing away at the victim from the inside trying to find a way out... And they often did.

'Rats dungeon' was yet another version of this torture used at the famed Tower of London around the Elizabethan era. A dark and dank room under the River Thames was used to house prisoners, they would be chained in place to the floor and left alone. The river's tide would rise which would fill the lower part of the room with water, then when the water receded, it would leave behind many disease-ridden and very hungry rats. The rats would then begin to eat the prisoners, by then, the prisoners began to have their 'flesh torn from the arms and legs' according to the book *The Pictorial History of England*. Not all prisoners were eaten alive by the rats, some would survive with bloody gaping wounds after having their skin eaten off, but they didn't last long as the diseases the rats carried would infect the prisoners and finally finish them off that way.

BOILING

Even more simplistic to understand than rat torture. I don't think there will be any major surprises in what boiling entailed (spoilers... It's boiling), but I feel there's still a good few titbits of info worth looking at regardless. It was in 1531 during the reign of King Henry VIII when Henry made this method a form of capital punishment for murder specifically committed by poison as the King had a deep-rooted fear of poisoning. Richard Roose, the cook for John Fisher, the then Bishop of Rochester, was found guilty and boiled alive when he confessed to poisoning the porridge eaten by several members of the household that killed two people in February of 1531.

Nobleman, William II de Soules was also boiled alive when he was found guilty of being involved in a conspiracy to kill Robert the Bruce in 1321 to become King of Scotland. But it's not just serious crimes where being boiled alive was the punishment, while crimes such as murder and treason were a certain way to meet the painful and gruesome death, smaller crimes such as theft and even forgery were a sure way to be boiled alive. In 1452, 1471 and even in 1687, several people were boiled alive for forging coins in Poland and Germany. Even Japan has used boiling when, in the 16th-century, a legendary bandit Ishikawa Goemon was given the brutal punishment when he attempted, but failed to kill warlord Toyotomi Hideyoshi. Goemon's punishment was particularly harrowing as not only was he boiled alive, but so was his entire family along with him. Goemon went on to become a popular culture icon particularity in Japan, but also around the world. You've most probably even seen traditional Japanese art depicting Ishikawa Goemon (and sometimes his family) being boiled alive.

Perhaps even more surprising is that boiling is reported as still used as punishment in the modern-day. The most recent confirmed use of the torture was from 2004 when Islam Karimov, the then leader of Uzbekistan, was known for boiling suspected terrorists. Even today, it has been suspected that ISIS has been known to boil prisoners alive in engine oil. Though no official reports have even been made. But it's not hard to believe that they very possibly used this torture method is it?

And yes, I did write being boiled alive in engine oil up there. The liquid used for this particular method of torture really seems to vary from culture to culture, year to year. Molten wax, various oils, molten lead, even wine and yes, the classic water, have all be used to boil people alive over the years. The traditional method would be to lower the victim into the boiling liquid feet first very slowly so they would witness and feel the slow and excruciating pain as their feet and legs would slowly dissolve. The skin, muscle and fat of their lower bodies would burn and fall off. Some people would die instantly of the shock and immeasurable pain, others managed to hold on until they were lowered even further in… I'm not sure which is worse. Another method would be to lower the victim in head-first. This resulted in a much more instant death as the head was boiled first. Perhaps the most cruellest of them all was to place the victim into the pot with the liquid cold and then have it heated up as they slowly awaited their fate. This method dragged the inevitable death out as long as possible as the victim felt the liquid gradually get hotter and hotter to the point of boiling as their flesh would slowly cook.

CATHERINE WHEEL

Also known as 'the breaking wheel', this was a much-used method of torture mainly used in Europe through the Middle Ages. This one has evolved and changed over the years. The earliest methods were really quite rudimentary and involved just tying someone to the outer rim of a large wooden wheel and then pushing it down a particularly steep and rocky hillside, where they would be bashed and crushed to death. Eventually, the wheel would be attached to an A-frame and controlled by a hand winch. Again, the victim would be tied to the outer rim only this time with something rather painful placed under the wheel, usually fire, metal spikes or similar. As the wheel was turned, the victim's body would revolve and be dragged slowly through the fire/spikes that would burn/cut the flesh of the person on the wheel. In some instances, spikes were even embedded into the rim of the wheel itself and the body of the victim lay on top of those too causing twice as much pain before their death.

One of the later versions of the Catherine wheel was very similar to crucifixion. The victim would have their arms and legs broken in various places, usually by being beaten multiple times with a metal pole. The broken limbs would then be threaded through the spokes of the wooden wheel and the victim tied firmly in place. The wheel would then be fixed to a sturdy and very tall pole, which would then be erected and left out in the hot sun for days. The victim could last for hours or even days in pain due to their broken limbs and the heat from the sun wouldn't do them any favours either. They would die in a similar manner to that of crucifixion... That's if the numerous crows that would land on the wheel and victim didn't peck them to death first.

The French also used a version similar to the previous one, only they didn't fix the wheel to a pole and effectively crucify their victims. Their version was even more brutal. They would build a wooden scaffold and the wheel would be attached to the top via a pole that fed through the scaffold that could be used to rotate the wheel underneath via manual labour. The wheel would slowly turn on top of the scaffold where one, sometimes two executioners armed with large and heavy metal hammers or iron bars, would take it in turns to hit each of the victim's limbs several times as they slowly rotated on the wheel, breaking multiple bones. This could be carried out for days and the victim would often die of shock and dehydration. But if they did manage to survive long enough, then the executioner(s) would be ordered to deliver a final and fatal blow, usually to the chest, known as a 'coups de grâce' (blow of mercy)... Which is where the phrase originates. The last known use of this version of the wheel was in August 1788 for the execution of Jean Louschart, who was thought to have been guilty of killing his own father. On the day of the execution, many supporters of Louschart, who learned he killed his father in self-defence due to excessive abuse, stormed the scaffold and freed the young man. King Louis XVI pardoned Jean Louschart and then abolished the use of the Catherine wheel as a method of torture and execution.

LINGCHI

This Chinese form of torture and death is a much more horrific and grisly version of flaying, and also known as 'death by a thousand cuts'. Said to have been first used as early as the 7th century before being outlawed in 1905... Though it had been reported as still being used even after being outlawed. This one was kept as punishment for severe crimes such as treason and murder.

The condemned prisoner would be stripped naked and then securely tied to a wooden frame or post and in public for all to see. They would then be slowly cut over and over with a blade. There was no set pattern to follow and the cuts would start anywhere on the body, though the chest was often the favoured starting point. But it wasn't just being cut over and over, as time went on those cuts became butchering. Chunks of flesh and muscle would be removed from the victim, even to the point of exposing bone. If the victim was still alive even after having pieces of their flesh and muscle cut off (many didn't), the torture would continue to the lower body. There are reports of people lasting anywhere between fifteen minutes to several hours with those who did live the longest managing to survive up to three thousand cuts before suffering a very painful death. But even after death, there was more to come as the victim would then be decapitated along with having their limbs removed. This form of dismemberment was used to punish the person even further in the afterlife as the victim would not be 'whole' in spiritual life after death.

For the finale of this particularly ghastly and morbid torture, I have a nice little bonus, I guess and a throwback to a previous chapter. The last officially known use of lingchi was to execute Fou-tchou-li (AKA, Fu-zhu-li) who was found guilty of murdering a prince in 1905. What's remarkable about this torture, in particular, is that it was actually caught on film, well in photos at least, yes even from 1905. The photos can be found very easily online too, all arranged into chronological order and complete with descriptions of the grisly torture and death. So yeah, if you want to see someone actually being killed via lingchi, it's surprisingly easy to find with a quick interwebs search. I'll let your morbid curiosity do the rest...

JUDAS CRADLE

The French called it 'la veille', the Germans preferred 'Judaswiege' and the Italians liked the name 'culla di Guida'. The Medieval English just called it Judas Cradle and it was horrendous. Designed to be both as painful and as humiliating as possible, this form of torture was similar to impalement, only much, much worse.

The main device used was a tall stool-like seat, at around six to seven-foot tall. But on top of the seat of the stool was a metal pyramid complete with a pointed end. The intended victim would be stripped naked with their arms tied behind their back, while their feet were bound together in front of them, which is already pretty uncomfortable... But it gets worse. The victim would then be secured to the walls/ceiling via a rope and pulley system and slowly lowered onto the metal, pointy 'seat' of the stool. Given the fact there was a sharpened pyramid at the top, as the victim was lowered, that pointed end would find it's way into the anus or vagina and begin to cause great pain and discomfort.

Often used as a way to gain information from the person being tortured. If they refused to talk, then the torturer would rock the victim, add brass weights to them, jiggle and jostle the legs of the stool and even raise then lower the victim suddenly via the pulley, to cause as much pain as possible, as the inserted pointed end of the pyramid would protrude the victim's cavity. Given the fact the legs of the victim were tied together, this would increase the pain as one leg could not move independently of the other. Sometimes oil was used to make 'access' more conformable, but this was not a sign of weakness or to show mercy on the part of the torturer. In fact, it was quite the opposite as it made the 'access' easier and allowed the torture to carry on much longer before the victim died.

The victims could be tortured for a few hours before the pain would kill them off, sometimes death would take several days. Some torturers would even use the pulley to raise the victim over the Judas Cradle and away from the pyramid, not to help the victim, but to leave them hanging over the device overnight or if they had passed out from the pain to give them time to recover and then continue with the torture in the following morning... If they hadn't bled to death in the meantime that is. Then there was the fact that the device was never cleaned between torture sessions, so if the wounds and pain of having a sharp point of a pyramid thrust into your anus multiple times didn't kill you, then the infections you'd most certainly get from previous victims blood would.

BLOOD EAGLE

This particularly bloody and violent torture method comes from Scandinavia from around the 8th-11th century, the time of Vikings. The victim would be secured in place and usually lying down chest to the floor in a prone position. The torturer would then use a sharpened tool, a knife, sword, etc to cut open the back of the victim... Yes, they were still alive too. The skin was then pulled back and muscle tissue was next to be cut open until the back of the ribcage was exposed.

Yes, the victim would still quite often be alive at this point. Also at this point, the torturer would rub salt in the wound… Literally. Grabbing handfuls of salt, they would rub it into the skin and muscle tissue to cause even more pain. Though I'm not really sure just how much more pain could be caused with salt if your back had been cut open to the ribcage. Anyway, if the victim was still alive, there was much worse to come. The ribs would be detached from the spine one by one and then pried open outwards making access to the lungs… And there's still more.

At this point, most victims would have died but for those that still hung onto life, there was one final stage. The lungs would be pulled out of the ribcage and spread over the opened ribs, over the back of the victim. The effect was said to look like an eagle spreading its wings, hence the name Blood Eagle. Traditionally this was done to the back, but some depictions via carvings show the torture being done to the front of the victim. A Blood Eagle was also said to have been done as a sacrificial offering to the Norse God Of War, Odin. Famed and feared Viking, Ivar the Boneless is said to have tortured and killed King Ælla of Northumbria using the Blood Eagle method after he previously killed Ivar's father.

HANGED, DRAWN AND QUARTERED

I don't know if it's actually possible to have a 'favourite' torture method, but this is mine. Now it time to get really nasty. This particular torture method was an extremely brutal manner to end someone's life which combined elements of other forms of torture to create one terribly agonizing and slow demise. The pain at the start was horrid and even after death, the victim's body was still brutalised further. An English punishment and means of death saved for males specifically, who were found guilty of high treason and used mainly in and around the 14th century, though it had been used before then too.

I could try to describe being hung, drawn and quartered myself… But I think this excerpt taken from *The Proceedings of the Old Bailey, 1674-1913* should cover it:

"Then Sentence was passed, as followeth, viz. That they should return to the place from whence they came, from thence be drawn to the Common place of Execution upon Hurdles, and there to be Hanged by the Necks, then cut down alive, their Privy-Members cut off, and Bowels taken out to be burned before their Faces, their Heads to be severed from their Bodies, and their Bodies divided into four parts, to be disposed of as the King should think fit."

Okay, so maybe a more layman/modern terminology is needed? Basically, you would be taken from the place of sentencing for your crime by horse. Only this was not a nice leisurely trot, you would be tied to a wooden panel, if lucky, which in turn was tied to a horse where you would then be, very uncomfortably and painfully, pulled to your place of execution. On arrival, you would then be hanged… But not to death, just very close to it. Still alive and struggling to breathe, you would then be placed on a table and tied down. The executioner would then cut open your belly and begin to remove your internal organs, but only the ones that you could live without, for a while at least, so you were still alive to witness the rest. This being a torture method exclusively for males led to the next part… The removal of the sexual organs, still alive at this point remember. Your recently removed internal organs, along with the meat and two veg, would then be thrown into a fire, placed in full view so you could see everything.

Then came the finale, oh yeah, there's more. Next up was the blow that would kill you off as the executioner used an axe to remove your head. But even then, after being dragged by a horse, hung to almost death, having your bowels removed along with your genitals… Which were then burnt while you watched and then being decapitated, even though at this point you were most definitely dead. There was still more. You would then finally be quartered, having your body cut into four pieces via vertical cuts through the spine and then removing the legs at the hip. All of this was done in full public view too. The body parts and head were then gathered up and par-boiled in a mixture of spices or sometimes tar to help preserve them because even after all of that, there was still further punishment to come. Your remains would then be displayed for all too see around the country and used as a warning against others who may think about betraying the Crown.

There were variations on this method, one included the quartering being done by tying the prisoner to four horses, which would then be made to quickly gallop away, pulling your body apart. Some reports state that the executioners carrying out the beheading and quartering elements were often very inexperienced. This led to some rather shoddy work such as not cleanly removing the head from the body and it needing multiple hacks to finally kill the prisoner. Or sometimes they'd even make a mess, or should that read, even more of a mess than needed to remove the internal organs causing unbelievable pain.

Some famed people given this horrific and merciless demise include Major-General Thomas Harrison on the 13th of October, 1660 who, while being cut open to have his bowels removed actually punched his executioner in the face. There was Guy Fawkes who was set to have been hung, drawn and quartered for his involvement in the infamous Gunpowder Plot of 1605. However, while being hanged during his torture on the 31st of January 1606, Fawkes, who had to watch the death of his fellow plotters via this torture method, managed to somehow get free and jumped or fell from the scaffold that the hanging was taking place on. Fawkes broke his neck and died instantly. Guy Fawkes may have escaped the pain and anguish of the rest of the torture, but his body was still quartered regardless, as was the custom, and put on display for all to see.

But perhaps the most famous person to have ever been hung, drawn and quartered was William Wallace, who met his fate on the 23rd of August 1305. After his trial at the Tower of London, he was dragged by horse to Smithfield where he was hanged, emasculated, eviscerated, beheaded and finally cut into four parts. His preserved head was placed on a spike on top of London Bridge. His quartered body was sent to be displayed in Newcastle, Berwick, Stirling, and Perth fro all to see as a warning for his involvement in the rebellious uprising against the English. Then to make things much, much worse, Mel Gibson played William Wallace in a film almost seven hundred years later… Nasty.

POENA CULLEI

What have the Romans ever done for us? Apart from sanitation, medicine, education, wine, public order, irrigation, roads, freshwater systems, and public health? Well, they created poena cullei or 'penalty of the sack'. Definitely used around 100 BC, but some historians claim it's possibly even older than that. This bizarre but effective form of torture was saved for a very specific crime, that of parricide. It also had a very specific and strange procedure.

The condemned prisoner, after their trial, would be forced to wear heavy wooden clogs and made to walk very uncomfortably through the town to a public area, while also wearing a bag over their head made from wolf-skin. The prisoner would then be tied down and viciously flogged/whipped with 'virgis sanguinis' (blood-coloured rods) until they bled profusely. After which, the commended would then be put into a large sack, usually made from ox-leather… But not put in the sack alone. Joining the now beaten and bloodied were a selection of animals, and not just random creatures either but very specifically chosen ones. A rooster, a dog, a monkey and a viper would be thrown into the sack too. The animals were specifically selected for symbolic reasons, which I will cover next. Largely explained by Gaius Plinius Secundus (Pliny the Elder), a Roman writer and nature philosopher.

So, the rooster was there as the Romans believed it was a very fierce animal, even more so than lions or tigers. The dog was seen as an impure and filthy beast, traits connected to the crime of parricide. Then a monkey was chosen as it represented the human being punished… Even though the human was already in the sack. Then finally, a viper because they believed that when this animal gave birth, the young tore through the belly, killing the parent, again symbolic of the crime that poena cullei was created for.

Anyway, so these angry and fierce animals were all thrown into the sack along with the guilty prisoner. The obvious would happen and the animals would start fighting, biting and clawing away at anything, including the victim's body. While this was going on, the sack would be dragged to the Tiber River and thrown in. The heavy wooden clogs worn by the victim would help weigh the sack down, along with the fact it had four angry, wild animals and a human in it too, and the sack would sink, drowning all inside. Though it has been suggested that most of the time, the victim died way before reaching the Tiber as the animals would usually tear the victim apart before then. A very strange, elaborate and cruel torture for sure, not just for the accused but also for the numerous animals who also died.

QUESTIONABLE CELEBRITY DEATHS

So, seeing as I did an opening chapter on celebrities who have killed, I thought I would end this book with a little balance. A final chapter on celebrities who have died... But whose death's still cast a black cloud of uncertainty on how/why they died. Whether the killer was never found, the celebrity died in strange/bizarre circumstances or some elements of the deaths just don't add up. The following celebrity deaths all share a common thread, the deaths have left many more questions than answers.

MARILYN MONROE

Born Norma Jeane Mortenson on the 1st of June, 1926. Coming from a difficult childhood, Mortenson was shy and reclusive. After holding down several menial jobs, Norma Mortenson signed up to a modelling agency in 1945 using the name Jean Norman, she straightened her naturally curly brown hair and dyed it blonde. After several modelling jobs, Mortenson signed a six-month contract with 20th Century-Fox executive, Ben Lyon. Between herself and Lyon, the two came up with a new stage name. It was Ben Lyon who chose the first name, Marilyn, after Broadway star Marilyn Miller, while Norma Mortenson came up with the last name, Monroe, her mother's maiden name. In August 1946, Marilyn Monroe was born.

Marilyn got her first film roles, bit parts in films like 1947's *Dangerous Years* and 1948's *Scudda Hoo! Scudda Hay!*. Struggling to get any big acting roles, Marilyn Monroe began to study acting, singing and dancing by attending classes. Monroe's teachers told her she was way too shy to be a star and that she should look for a new job. Marilyn Monroe was shy, but also very strong-headed. Despite her naysayers, Monroe refused to quit acting and after a few more bit parts in a handful of films, she became one of the biggest, most recognised, influential and famous actresses on the planet. Marilyn Monroe really does not need an introduction, does she? Her rise to fame in the 1950s thanks to films like *Gentlemen Prefer Blondes*, *There's No Business Like Show Business*, *The Seven Year Itch* and *Some Like It Hot* made her one of the most sought after actresses working in Hollywood. Her fame and popularity were insane and Marilyn Monroe is still seen as a cultural icon today.

BOOK OF DEATHS

She was riding high on the wave of success and fame through the 1950s and into the early 1960s. The shy and quiet Norma Jeane Mortenson was dead and the loud, sexy, confident and much-lauded Marilyn Monroe was very much alive... Even if only for a few years.

In the early hours of the morning on the 5th of August, 1962, Monroe's housekeeper called her psychiatrist after getting no response from the movie star in her room. The psychiatrist also failed to get a response, and so broke into Marilyn Monroe's room via a window, when he then found her dead body lying naked on her bed at her Los Angeles home. Marilyn Monroe was pronounced dead at 4:25 AM, but reports state she died sometime between 8:30 PM and 10:30 PM the previous night. Marilyn Monroe was aged just 36 when she died. There was no indication of foul play and her death was ruled as 'probable suicide' given the toxicology report showing acute barbiturate poisoning. Still, many people believe she was murdered.

But why, who would want to kill the most famous and very much loved actress on the planet at the time? Well, it has been a pretty open secret that Marilyn Monroe liked her men... A lot. She was married three times in her life and was known to have had several extramarital affairs too. It was an affair she supposedly had with a couple of brothers that many people think led to her untimely death. It has been strongly suggested that Monroe was having an affair with, not only the then President of the United States, John F. Kennedy, but also his brother, Robert F. Kennedy. Conspiracy theorists have long suggested that Marilyn Monroe was killed to prevent her from spilling any secrets about the Kennedy brothers. There are several CIA files and reports that can be found on the CIA.gov website covering Monroe's death... Many of them have been 'sanitised for the public' (edited and censored) to read. Still, seen as an icon almost sixty years after her death, I guess Marilyn Monroe's candle burned out long before her legend ever will.

NATALIE WOOD

At around 8 AM on the 29th of November, 1981, the body of 43-year-old actress Natalie Wood washed up on a beach of Santa Catalina Island, off the coast of Southern California. The reasons for her death are still questioned even today. Wood was a child star with a semi-successful career in TV as a teenager. As an adult, her movie career including films like *Rebel Without a Cause* and *The Searchers*, really got her noticed. But it was Natalie Wood's role as Maria in W*est Side Story* from 1961 when her career really took off and she began to get noticed in Hollywood.

Natalie Wood married actor Robert Wagner in 1957, though their relationship didn't last and they divorced in 1962. After another failed marriage, Wood and Wagner rekindled their relationship in 1972 and remarried. In 1981, Natalie Wood started work on her latest film, *Brainstorm*. During a break in production, she took a weekend trip to Santa Catalina Island on-board her husband's yacht, Splendour. Also on the yacht were her husband, Robert Wagner, Natalie Wood's co-star on the film, Christopher Walken and the captain of the yacht, Dennis Davern. So how did Wood go from enjoying a boat trip on the night of 28th of November, 1981 to washing up dead on a beach a few hours later?

The original ruling of Natalie Wood's death was an accidental drowning and hypothermia. A small dinghy was also washed up on the beach where Wood's body was found. An autopsy report revealed that she had a blood alcohol content of 0.14%, given the limit for driving a car legally was 0.10%, she could've been described as being drunk at the time of her death. Then there was the fact that there were traces of motion-sickness and painkiller pills in her bloodstream, both of which would increase the effects of the alcohol. So her death was seen as accidental, possibly due to the booze and mixing with over-the-counter drugs. The county coroner at the time suggested that Natalie Wood fell into the water while struggling in the dinghy out at sea. But there were issues with that ruling…

The first question raised was why Natalie Wood would've been in a small dinghy floating around the North Pacific Ocean instead of being on-board her husband's yacht? Other doubts came about when Wood's sister, Lana claimed that Natalie couldn't swim and had a lifelong fear of the water, so very much doubted she would even get into the dinghy to begin with. Two witnesses on another boat at the time also claimed that they heard a woman screaming for help that night. Robert Wagner claimed that his wife stayed up after he went to bed so could not say how she ended up falling into the sea as he was asleep. The autopsy report also revealed that Natalie Wood had several bruises on her body and arms, as well as an abrasion on her left cheek, but no indication as to how or when they occurred. It was doubtful that falling out of a dinghy into the sea would've caused the injures. So even though her death was ruled as accidental, there were doubts for decades.

The case was reopened in 2011 when the captain of the yacht, Dennis Davern publicly claimed that he previously lied to police when originally questioned and later stated that he witnessed Robert Wagner grow angry with his wife because she was flirting with Christopher Walken on the yacht. According to Davern, he was on deck and could hear the couple's loud arguing, he went to their cabin to check on them only to be told to go away (only not that politely) by Wagner. He also said that the argument continued above deck and that the couple stormed off to the back of the yacht and out of his sight, where the argument continued for while before it all went quiet. This was when Davern went to check on them again, this time finding Wagner alone when, according to Davern, Wagner said:

"Natalie's gone. She's missing".

Dennis Davern also claimed that once it was discovered that Natalie Wood was no longer on the yacht, that Robert Wagner refused to allow him to turn on the searchlights or notify authorities.

In 2012, Natalie Wood's death certificate was amended and her cause of death was changed from 'accidental drowning' to 'drowning and other undetermined factors'. Other amendments also include how the circumstances surrounding exactly how Wood ended up in the water as not clearly established. Plus a ten-page addendum to Wood's autopsy report states that the bruises and injures found on her body were perhaps sustained before she fell into the sea, not after or by falling in as originally thought, and that she was most probably assaulted before she drowned. During this re-investigation, Christopher Walken hired a lawyer, fully cooperated with the police and was ruled out of being a suspect. In 2018, Robert Wagner was named as a person of interest in the re-investigation into Natalie Wood's death, though he has denied any involvement in his wife's death. The case continues…

S. L. PERRIN

GEORGE REEVES

Good looking, charming and chisel-jawed actor George Reeves (born George Brewer) began his acting career in 1939 in the classic epic, *Gone with the Wind*, in a minor, 'blink and you'll miss it' role. He had a few more bit parts and a handful larger ones over the years in several B-movies, acting alongside the likes of Ronald Reagan and James Cagney. Struggling to find major roles, Reeves put his acting career on hold and enlisted in the US Army, he was drafted for service in 1943. After World War II ended, George Reeves was discharged and he decided to pick up his acting career once more. He still struggled to find suitable movie roles or get noticed as a serious actor, so he decided to turn his talent to TV and radio instead of films, a move that would catapult him to stardom.

It was 1951 when George Reeves was offered the main role in a then-new TV show based on the DC comic book superhero, Superman in *Adventures of Superman*. First shooting what would be used as both a B-movie and pilot for the TV show, *Superman and the Mole Men*, the first-ever on-screen appearance of Superman. The movie and TV show became a big hit and Reeves, in turn, became a big Hollywood star. Through the mid to late fifties, George Reeves was making a lot of money for his Superman role as well as other acting jobs, but he could never escape the shadow of Superman no matter how many times he tried... And he tried a lot.

On the 15th of June, 1959, Reeves had been out for diner with Leonore Lemmon, his fiancée. Joining the couple were writer, Robert Condon. After diner and drinks, the trio headed to George Reeves' Beverly Hills home for a small party. They were joined at the house by two neighbours, William Bliss and Carol Van Ronkel. It was around midnight when Reeves decided to go to bed. However, the small party was creating noise and the Superman star soon went back downstairs and complained about the commotion. Despite wanting to go to sleep, Reeves stayed up with his guests a little while longer, had a drink before returning upstairs to his bedroom. Shortly after, sometime around 2:00 AM on the 16th of June, 1959, a single gunshot was heard. One of the guests, William Bliss ran upstairs to investigate the noise and found a naked George Reeves dead, lying on his back on his bed with his feet still on the floor, and a .30 calibre Luger pistol between his feet. It looked and sounded like a simple case of suicide, and that was the official ruling too... But it wouldn't be in this book if it was that simple.

Several questions and mysteries are still unanswered surrounding George Reeves' death. No one called the police after discovering Reeves' body, at least not for a few hours. When the police did arrive, they noted that the four witnesses were very drunk and their stories didn't match up when questioned. A news report taken from the Sarasota Journal on the 17th of June, 1959 states that Leonore Lemmon (after Reeves returned to his bedroom) said to the other guests:

"He is going to shoot himself. He is getting the gun out now and he is going to shoot himself."

Then after the gunshot sounded, Lemmon reportedly said:

"See there, I told you."

Leonore Lemmon was said to have been as calm as anything as if she knew George Reeves was planning on killing himself... Or if she knew someone was going to kill him. But, another source claims that, after hearing the gunshot, Lemmon came running downstairs and reportedly said:

"Tell them I was down here, tell them I was down here."

Suggesting that Leonore Lemmon was in the bedroom when George Reeves was shot. Even friends and family said that Reeves showed no signs of depression, he was known to love life and would never have taken his own. Reeves also left no note to suggest he wanted to commit suicide. The house was sealed by police for the investigation, but during the night, the police evidence seal on the house had been broken and $4000 in cash taken from the property... Leonore Lemmon also disappeared and it's assumed she disappeared with the missing money.

The gun that was found at George Reeves' feet had no fingerprints on it, not even Reeves'. There was also no gunpowder residue on his hands either. So how could he have shot himself in the head to then afterwards clean the gun for fingerprints and also wash his hands of any gunpowder residue if he was dead? The bullet that killed George Reeves was recovered from the ceiling of his bedroom, but the casing of the bullet was found under his body, lying on the bed. So how could a bullet casing land on the bed behind George and end up under his body if he shot himself in the head from the front and fell backwards on to the bed? There were also two other bullets found stuck in the bedroom floor, meaning a total of three shots must have been fired and all three were confirmed to have been shot from the same gun too. Yet the witnesses that night say they only heard a single shot. Witness stories didn't match up, the evidence didn't make sense and yet, George Reeves' death was still ruled as a simple suicide. There's more…

At the hight of his Superman fame and before his relationship with Leonore Lemmon, George Reeves had a secret affair with Toni Mannix. Toni was the wife of Eddie Mannix who was the then general manager of the huge movie studio, Metro-Goldwyn-Mayer. It was Reeves who ended their relationship and it has been said that Toni resented him for it too. It had also been suggested that Eddie Mannix had some possible Mafia connections. Before she died in 1989, Toni in the presence of publicist Edward Lozzi confessed to a Catholic priest that she was the one who was responsible for George Reeves being killed. Still feeling hurt over being dumped by the Superman actor, Toni supposedly told her husband about the affair and he had a hitman kill George Reeves.

The 2006 film *Hollywoodland* tells the story of George Reeves (played by Ben Affleck), his fame via Superman and his eventual death. The film concludes with three possible endings. An accidental shooting at the hands of Leonore Lemmon, a murder by an unnamed hitman under orders from Eddie Mannix and the officially ruled suicide. Given the fact that all those attached to this mystery are now dead themselves, the truth about George Reeves' questionable death may never be known.

JILL DANDO

Crimewatch was a long-running show on British TV, who's aim it was to help solve various real crimes reported around the country. Originally, it began airing in 1984 and ended in 2017. The show was famed for its reconstructions of real-life crimes which were used to help gain information from the general public to assist in capturing the guilty parties. Over the years, *Crimewatch* featured many very high profile investigations including the murder of James Bulger, the disappearance of Madeleine McCann and the murders of Holly Wells and Jessica Chapman to name just a few. But there was one major crime featured on the show that was never solved and one very close to the hearts of the *Crimewatch* team themselves.

Nick Ross and Sue Cook co-presented the show together from its very first episode until Cook left in 1995. Brought in to replace Sue was journalist, newsreader and TV presenter Jill Dando. Dando was murdered, aged 37 years-old on the 26th of April, 1999. Her case was reconstructed for the very TV show she once presented after her brutal killing. Even today, whoever killed Jill Dando has never been caught and no one even knows why she was killed to begin with either.

After spending the morning shopping, Jill Dando returned to her home in Fulham, South West London at around 11:32 AM. Just as she was about to put her keys into the door, someone grabbed her from behind and forced her to the ground so her head was almost touching the steps of her porch. The killer held a 9mm calibre semi-automatic pistol in one hand, while they forced Dando's head closer to the step with the other. The killer then pushed the gun against Jill Dando's left temple and squeezed the trigger. The bullet entered her head and exited the other side, killing her instantly.

One of Dando's neighbours, Richard Hughes says he heard a surprised scream but no gunshot. After hearing the scream, Hughes looked out of the window and saw a six-foot-tall white man, aged around 40-years-old or so who was hurrying away from Jill Dando's house but thought nothing of it at the time. It was about fourteen minutes later at 11:46 when another neighbour, Helen Doble, walked home and discovered Jill Dando's dead body lying at her own front door. Doble recalled the scene in an interview:

"I was walking up the road and saw her car. I made a deliberate point of looking at her front door and in one step everything changed because I saw the most horrific thing. She was lying in a strange position and there was a lot of blood. At first I thought she had been stabbed or attacked.

Her hand was blue and from the way she looked I knew she was dead. It all looked very professional."

Jill Dando's murder kick-started one of the biggest manhunts in British crime history, even bigger than the hunt for the infamous Yorkshire Ripper in the seventies and eighties. The police investigation team spoke to more than two and a half thousand people and took well over one thousand statements in the first six months alone. Despite the investigation and even after a reconstruction was made on *Crimewatch*, the very show Dando presented when she was murdered, no one was ever found guilty of the crime... Well, there was Barry George.

Barry George lived fairly close to Jill Dando's home, he had a history of stalking women and numerous sexual offences in the past. After being put under surveillance, George was arrested and charged with Dando's murder in 2000. He went on trial and was sentenced to life in prison in July 2001. However, after three appeals, he was acquitted in 2008. They just didn't have a strong enough case, there was no solid evidence and no witnesses who could identify Barry George either, even though he did match the vague description of the man Richard Hughes saw hurrying away fro Jill Dando's home at the time. All they really had was his criminal past and the fact he lived nearby and that was just not enough to convict Barry George of murder.

There have been numerous theories surrounding the reasons for Jill Dando's death and her possible killer. A jealous ex-boyfriend was one possibility for a while, as Dando had begun a relationship and became engaged before she was killed. The fact no one heard the gunshot suggested a suppressor/silencer was used and the style in which she was murdered seemed very professional. So the possibility that a hitman was hired to kill her by someone who had been convicted due to her *Crimewatch* show was another theory. A stalker/deranged fan was another angle that was explored, but nothing ever came of it. Then there was the idea that it could've been a simple case of mistaken identity, but the fact Jill Dando was murdered on her own doorstep made that seem highly unlikely. Even now, over twenty years since her murder, no one has ever been arrested or charged and it's not even known why Jill Dando was murdered in the first place.

BOOK OF DEATHS

BRITTANY MURPHY & SIMON MONJACK

She was young, beautiful and talented. Brittany Murphy had a steady TV and film career through the nineties, appearing in various shows and slowly making name for herself. Perhaps her most famous TV role was in the animated show, *King of the Hill*, where she voiced both Joseph Gribble from 1997 to 2000 and Luanne Platter for the entire run of the show. Her breakthrough film was the 1995 teen comedy *Clueless*. More film roles followed including *Girl, Interrupted*, *8 Mile*, *Sin City* and *Happy Feet*. By the time the late 2000s came around, Brittany Murphy was becoming a notable Hollywood star.

In May 2007, Brittany Murphy married British screenwriter, film director and producer Simon Monjack and they moved into their Hollywood Hills home. After an evening of Thai food and watching movies, Murphy said that she felt ill, she had been complaining about flu-like symptoms for the previous few days. On the morning of the 20th of December, 2009, Brittany Murphy went to the bathroom and collapsed at around 8 AM. Emergency services were called and they tried to resuscitate Murphy at the scene, she was rushed to Cedars-Sinai Medical Center, but died aged 32 at 10:04 AM. after going into cardiac arrest.

Brittany Murphy's death was originally ruled as natural causes. In February 2010 the Los Angeles County coroner said that the primary cause of her death was pneumonia and iron-deficiency anaemia. Several drugs were also found in her system, but they were legal, over-the-counter prescription medication. However, the drugs were said to have been a factor in the death as they would've helped to exacerbate Murphy's already weakened state at the time. The official ruling into Brittany Murphy's death was accidental and that was that… For a few months.

On the 23rd of May, 2010, just five months after Brittany Murphy's death, her husband, Simon Monjack also unexpectedly died aged 40. At first, it was thought his death was suicide, most probably brought on from the grief over the loss of his wife, but it wasn't. Not only did Monjack die in the very same house that Murphy did just a few months before, but the coroner's report revealed the cause of death was pneumonia and severe anaemia, the same cause of death attributed to Brittany Murphy herself. Two people dying the exact same way in the same house just months apart? The natural causes/accidental death ruling seemed unlikely.

Brittany Murphy's mother claimed in 2011 that the deaths were brought on by toxic mould found in the home. But the Los Angeles County Department of Health found no evidence of such mould during an investigation. Some suggest that they were possibly poisoned as high levels of barium (a chemical used in some rat poison) was found in Murphy's hair during an independent toxicology investigation, but this was explained away by the fact that Brittany Murphy dyed her hair and that some dyes contained barium peroxide. Arsenic poisoning can often be confused with anaemia, which is was one of the factors in both deaths, so could it be possible they were killed with arsenic? But that would raise the question of who or why would anyone want to kill Brittany Murphy and Simon Monjack?

American forensic pathologist Dr. Cyril Wecht (who also worked on the JFK assassination case) said it would be extremely rare that two people would die of the exact same natural causes in the same house. Not impossible, but certainly very, very rare. Despite the questions surrounding both deaths, the unlikelihood of two people dying the exact same way just months apart, the possible poisoning angle, the case has never been reopened for investigation and the natural causes/accidental death ruling is the official stance.

PRINCESS DIANA

Well, I started this chapter with a candle in the wind, so may as well end with one too. Very easily one of the most shocking and most hardest to believe celebrity deaths ever, that shocked the entire planet... If not the most, Diana Frances Spencer. At one time, Diana, Princess of Wales was easily the most recognisable, famous and revered woman on the globe. She was shot into the limelight after her marriage to Charles, Prince of Wales in July 1981, Spencer went on to become the most popular member of the British royal family. Everything about her life was just so... Fairytale.

BOOK OF DEATHS

Diana Spencer was originally a very shy person and this would show during early interviews with the press. However, over the years, she gained a lot of self-confidence through her royal duties and toured the globe raising awareness of HIV/AIDS, landmines, cancer, homelessness, drug abuse, along with many other great causes. Her work with those less fortunate transformed her from that shy princess into one of the most respected ambassadors on the planet. Diana Spencer was soon cemented as 'The People's Princess' and became a public and style icon adored by millions and millions of people around the world.

But, behind the scenes, the fairytale relationship and life with Prince Charles was in serious trouble. Only five years into the marriage and the cracks began to show. Charles rekindled his relationship with his former girlfriend, Camilla Parker Bowles, while Diana herself had an affair with Major James Hewitt. The never-ending, constant media attention and speculation didn't help much either and she soon found herself facing depression, anxiety and bulimia. In November 1995, Diana Spencer gave a very candid interview to Martin Bashir for the BBC where she famously said:

"Well, there were three of us in this marriage, so it was a bit crowded."

On the 28th of August, 1996 Charles and Diana eventually divorced and just over a year later on the 31st of August, 1997, Diana Spencer was dead.

Being rushed away from the hounding paparazzi chasing on bikes, Spencer was in a car being driven by Henri Paul. Also in the car were Spencer's bodyguard Trevor Rees-Jones and her new lover, Dodi Fayed, The car was speeding away through the Pont de l'Alma tunnel in Paris when Paul lost control of the vehicle at 12:23 AM. Travelling at around sixty-five miles per hour (just over twice the speed limit), the car hit the right side wall of the tunnel and then swerved to the left, before smashing head-on into a stone support pillar of the tunnel. The car spun around and hit the wall of the tunnel backwards before stopping, causing substantial damage to the car. Everyone on board died except for Diana Spencer's bodyguard, Trevor Rees-Jones who survived the horrific crash with serious injuries.

An inquest into the tragedy ruled that the driver, Henri Paul was drunk at the time of the crash and that anti-depressants and anti-psychotic drugs were also found in his system. A verdict of unlawful killing through grossly negligent driving was to blame for the deaths and was put fully on Henri Paul. Case closed. However, some people feel that's not strictly true and still believe there are a few questions that have not been answered.

Theories range from the royal family not liking the fact Diana Spencer had started a relationship with Dodi Fayed, an Egyptian Muslim and that the couple had arranged to announce that they were going to marry. So some say that the crash was arranged to happen with the help of MI6 at the request of Prince Philip. Another theory claims that Spencer was pregnant with Fayed's child at the time of her death, a claim backed up by Dodi Fayed's father, Mohamed Al-Fayed. Supposedly, the royal family didn't want a Muslim baby in the family, so they had Diana Spenser killed. Though it has to be said that the autopsy of Spenser's body after her death proved she wasn't actually pregnant... But whoever arranged the crash (if they did) wouldn't have known that at the time. Plus, if a deadly car crash could be 'arranged', then surely so could a false autopsy? Then there was the lack of CCTV footage of the actual crash too. It was revealed that there were around fourteen CCTV cameras near the Pont de l'Alma tunnel where the crash occurred... Yet there was no usable evidence of the crash itself. It was reported that most of the cameras were facing the entrances to various buildings and not the road, so nothing usable was recorded. However, there was a specific traffic-monitoring camera placed directly above the entrance to the tunnel the crash happened in just to record footage of cars entering and exiting the tunnel, but there was still nothing recorded on it. It was reported that the department that ran that particular camera closed down at about 11 PM, over an hour before the fatal crash... Which certainly is convenient.

But, just how could the royal family, via MI6, orchestrate a million to one crash with the goal of killing someone? The chances of a certain death must have been extremely slim. This is where another theory comes in. Witnesses at the time say they saw a white Fiat Uno exit the tunnel after the crash that killed Diana Spencer. Not only that, but traces of white paint were said to have been found on the car that Spencer was in. It has been suggested that the Fiat Uno was being driven by a member of MI6 and drove into the path of the car being driven by Henri Paul, this is what caused Paul to initially lose control of the car as he swerved to try and avoid a crash. The driver of the white Fiat Uno was never officially found, or perhaps it is more accurate to say that they were never looked for to begin with? But the official ruling into the death of Diana Spencer is unlawful killing through grossly negligent driving with the blame put fully on the driver, Henri Paul.

FAMOUS VERY CLOSE & SAME DAY DEATHS

This is a little bonus chapter (not listed in the contents). I thought about including this originally, but left it out of the initial print of the book as I felt three chapters covering celebrity/famous related deaths was perhaps, a bit too much. Plus I thought this chapter was a little too long overall and it just felt a little uneven at the time too. But, seeing as I sat down to do this re-edit to correct a few mistakes and tidy up the formatting, and as I had this chapter doing nothing but sitting around on my hard-drive taking up space, I thought I'd throw it in at the end here just for fun.

Anyway, as the title suggests, this chapter looks at various famous names through history who have died on the same day (or very close to), often (unintentionally) stealing the limelight and major press from each other while sometimes also creating some strange and interesting coincidences along the way.

4th OF JULY, 1826

The 4th of July, the day the Declaration of Independence of the United States is celebrated. BBQs, fireworks, political speeches and the like fill the day as Yanks celebrate their independence, as well they should too. The Declaration of Independence of 1776 was worked on by several of the Founding Fathers of the United States. A group of highly respected leaders who quite literally untied the states of America after the whole 'unpleasantness' with us Brits. The Founding Fathers were made up of seven men: John Adams, Benjamin Franklin, Alexander Hamilton, John Jay, Thomas Jefferson, James Madison, and George Washington. Between those seven, they created the foundations on which the USA was built on. Several of those Founding Fathers went on to create the Declaration of Independence and of those men, two of them died on the same day, fifty years to the day after creating the very document that secured America's independence.

John Adams served as the second POTUS and died on the 4th of July, 1826 aged 90 years-old. Adams' final words before his death have been reported as being:

180

BOOK OF DEATHS

"Thomas Jefferson survives."

A reference to his friend and fellow Founding Father. Jefferson was the third POTUS after Adams. However, unbeknown to John Adams, Thomas Jefferson had actually died just a few hours before aged 83. Two former Presidents, Founding Fathers and writers of the Declaration of Independence both dying on the very day they created fifty years earlier.

30th OF JANUARY, 1948

Orville Wright, along with his brother Wilbur, are names anyone with an ounce of historical knowledge should instantly recognise. I mean, the Wright brothers did essentially create modern aviation when they built the Wright Flyer in 1903. As mentioned by the Smithsonian National Air and Space Museum:

> "On December 17, 1903, at Kitty Hawk, North Carolina, the Wright Flyer became the first powered, heavier-than-air machine to achieve controlled, sustained flight with a pilot aboard."

One of the most important technological discoveries, which opened the entire world to air travel. This discovery also bought about the invention of planes to be used for war. Of course, Orville Wright had no idea that his part in creating human flight in 1903 would lead to the ability to drop a nuclear bomb and more. And when Wright died of a heart attack on the 30th of January, 1948 aged 78, he passed on the same day as someone as far removed from war as you can get. One of the most, if not THE most famous pacifists, anti-colonial nationalists and political ethicists ever also died. Mohandas Karamchand Gandhi, or Mahatma Gandhi as he was more commonly known as, was shot and killed by Nathuram Godse. Gandhi, 78 was on his way to address a prayer meeting at the then called, Birla House in New Delhi, India when Godse fired three rounds from a pistol into Gandhi's chest. Some accounts state that Gandhi died instantly, others suggest he was carried into a bedroom in Birla House and died around thirty minutes later. Either way, one man who (inadvertently) helped forge the path of war and one who did any and everything he could to avoid it, both died on the 30th of January, 1948.

181

10th & 11th OF OCTOBER, 1963

The name Jean Cocteau isn't one that'll you'll probably recognise... Unless you really know your French history. Cocteau was a much loved and respected poet, novelist, artist, film-maker, actor, singer and fashion designer in his homeland of France. He also had a rather unhealthy obsession with a name you should recognise, young songbird Edith Piaf, also from France. In 1940, Cocteau actually wrote a play for Piaf and her then-husband, Paul Meurisse, called *Le bel indifférent* (*The Beautiful Indifferent*). The play (later turned into a short film) basically tells the tale of a woman who doubts her husband after she feels he has wronged her. Edith Piaf performed the play with Paul Meurisse and it was a spectacular flop. At the time, Piaf wasn't really known, she was a young talent that couldn't get a breakthrough. In fact, the play is credited with ending her marriage... which some people have suggested was Jean Cocteau's intention all along.

Anyway, it was the early fifties when Jean Cocteau, still obsessing over Edith Piaf, saw her performing in a Parisian backstreet dive of a place. The still respected critic then wrote an article about her performance, which helped to finally launch her career proper. After which, Cocteau and Piaf became close friends. Edith Piaf went on to international success, most famed for the song *Non, je ne regrette rien* (*No, I do not regret anything*). However, Piaf began to use and abuse alcohol and various pain relief medications and her health began to deteriorate. Edith Piaf died on the 10th of October, 1963. She was just 47-years-old. Just a few hours later and after hearing of the news that Edith Piaf had died, Jean Cocteau reportedly said:

> "Ah, la Piaf est morte. Je peux mourir aussi."
> ("Ah, Piaf's dead. I can die too.")

And so he did, aged 74. Cocteau died of a heart attack just minutes after uttering his final words and only a few hours following the death of Piaf. As respected as Jean Cocteau was, especially in France, his death is often overlooked as over forty thousand Edith Piaf fans flooded the streets and mobbed her funeral, while Jean Cocteau's funeral was a much quieter and underwhelming affair.

BOOK OF DEATHS

22nd OF NOVEMBER, 1963

Two very famous and much loved British writers both died on the same day, the 22nd of November, 1963. Aldous Huxley wrote nearly fifty books, as well as various essays, narratives, and poems. Huxley was nominated for the Nobel Prize in Literature seven times and had several of his works turned into movies. Perhaps his most famous book was the dystopian social science fiction novel, *Brave New World*. Which itself has seen numerous radio, TV and movie adaptations over the years. C. S. Lewis was the second of the two famed British writers to die on the same day. Does C. S. Lewis really need an introduction? I mean, he did pen *The Chronicles of Narnia* series of books. You know, Aslan the lion, the Pevensie kids, Mr. Tumnus, Prince Caspian and all those memorable characters. Seven books in total, just for the Narnia series alone, if you wanted to know. Anyway, that's two massively popular British writers who died on the same day of the 22nd of November, 1963. However, as famed as both Aldous Huxley and C. S. Lewis were, their sad deaths were massively overshadowed by someone else who died on the same day. Some American fella who went out for a ride in a car, down Elm Street in Dallas, Texas.

John F. Kennedy was the 35th president of the United States and was on a political trip to smooth out frictions in the Democratic Party. Kennedy was loved by a great many... except for one man who shot him as he travelled through Dallas in an open-top Lincoln Continental. Lee Harvey Oswald was hiding out in the now famed Texas School Book Depository, where he fired three shots at JFK's presidential motorcade. The President was hit twice, once in the back and once in the head. I'm not going to get into conspiracy theories, the Warren Commission, grassy knolls, Zapruder film, umbrella man or any of that guff. Lee Harvey Oswald alone killed JFK, and on the same day as two British writers too.

16th OF SEPTEMBER 1977

Maria Callas was an opera singer... that is perhaps, a gross understatement. Callas was one of the finest opera singers to have ever lived and was often called La Divina (the Divine one). Maria Callas was most probably best known for her performances of the opera, *Madama Butterfly*. Later in her life, Callas fell into a pit of depression after a particularly tumultuous relationship with millionaire businessman Aristotle Onassis, and when Onassis died in 1975, her depression got increasingly worse. Callas became a recluse, locker her self away at her home in Paris. She would smoke, drink and take sleeping pills and painkillers, soon becoming addicted. On the morning of the 16th of September, 1977, Maria Callas was served breakfast in bed and after eating, she fell unconscious and died of a heart attack aged 53.

Later that same day in London and glam rock band T-Rex frontman, Marc Bolan, was being driven a Mini 1275GT by American singer, Gloria Jones. Bolan never learned to drive as he had an irrational fear of cars, so much so that he even said he thought he would die in a car crash. Even more so, Bolan was a big fan of James Dean who died when he crashed his 'Little Bastard' Porsche. In the documentary film, *Marc Bolan: Cosmic Dancer*, record producer Simon Napier-Bell said:

> "Chet Baker was a hero of his, and James Dean. And I said, 'Well, be careful having James Dean as a hero, because you might end up dying in a Porsche. And he said, 'Oh, I'm just tiny, I'd like to die in a Mini.'"

And that's exactly what happened too. The Mini Marc Bolan was in, being driven by Gloria Jones, hit a steel-reinforced fence post before smashing into a sycamore tree. While Jones escaped with a few broken bones, Bolan, 29 was killed. Two famed musical stars both dying on the same day.

10th OF OCTOBER, 1985

Aside from managing to fool a few people that aliens had invaded Earth with his famed *The War of the Worlds* radio broadcast in 1938, Orson Welles was a talented man. Actor, director, screenwriter and producer who often pushed boundaries and film-making in general. I mean... *Citizen Kane*. Welles was a true inventor and often considered as one of the most important and greatest film-makers ever. In his later life, Orson Welles became a little bit 'weird' and (famously) he developed quite an inflated ego too, Welles also really enjoyed his drink and cigars. Wells died aged 70, of a heart attack on the morning of the 10th of October, 1985.

184

BOOK OF DEATHS

Just a few hours later that same day and some Russian fella died, and another fella who liked to smoke too. Russian born Yul Brynner became an American film icon in his time and starred in numerous big and much-loved flicks. Brynner had been diagnosed with lung cancer in 1983 and died two years later, just a few hours after Orson Welles. What's interesting about Yul Brynner's lung cancer was that he actually decided to take part in an anti-smoking campaign filmed before his death. However, it wasn't shown until after he had died. In the short clip, Brynner delivers a message from beyond the grave by saying:

"Now that I'm gone, I tell you, don't smoke. Whatever you do, just don't smoke. If I could take back that smoking, we wouldn't be talking about any cancer. I'm convinced of that."

16th OF MAY, 1990

Sammy Davis Jr. was known as one of the greatest entertainers to ever exist. Singer, dancer, actor, vaudevillian, writer and comedian, Davis started his career aged just 3-years-old. But it was in the sixties when he really made his mark, mainly for becoming part of the famed Rat Pack group of entertainers with the lies of Frank Sinatra and Dean Martin. While fighting against the racism and segregation of the time, Sammy Davis Jr. still managed to become a bona fide star. In fact, it was Davis' popularity and his own determined grit that actually helped to break down the race barrier often found in the entertainment industry back then. Like so many others back then, Sammy Davis Jr. was a heavy smoker and drinker, and doctors found a cancerous tumour in his throat in 1989. Davis died following complications from his throat cancer on the 16th of May, 1990. But earlier that day, one of my personal heroes also died.

I'm not someone who's easily impressed by fame. Meeting celebrities isn't something I'm particularity interested in, but if there is one (group) of entertainers I'd love to meet, it would be The Muppets. I grew up watching those zany marionette-puppets created by Jim Henson and still love them forty years later as an adult. Henson created one of the greatest brands ever with his Muppets. Of course, he was also famed for his films and TV shows as a writer, producer, director and even actor. With *Labyrinth* being one of my all-time favourite films. Still, Jim

185

Henson began to worry himself over a sore throat he had had for a good while, but chose to ignore in favour of working on new projects. In the early hours of the 15th of May, 1990, Henson was having trouble breathing and began to cough up blood. Jim Henson was taken to hospital shortly later, stopped breathing and was rushed to intensive care. X-rays showed that Henson had developed multiple abscesses on both of his lungs following a previous bacterial infection. He was placed on a ventilator and given strong antibiotics, which did kill off most of the infection, but the damage had already been done to his internal organs. Jim Henson held on for most of the day but died at 1:21 AM on the 16th of May, 1990 aged 53. It was later revealed that if Jim Henson had gotten treatment just a few hours earlier, or if he had gone to the doctors when he first began to worry about his sore throat, he would've survived.

24th OF NOVEMBER, 1991

My musical tastes are quite eclectic. I really do enjoy a good mix of musical styles from pretty much any decade, but I do have a particular soft spot for rock music and on the 24th of November, 1991, the world lost two wild rockers. Paul Charles Caravello was better known as Eric Carr, the drummer for rock band Kiss. Early 1991 and Carr began to feel rather ill, medical tests showed that he had heart cancer. Carr had several surgeries to remove tumours in his right atrium and lungs to try and prevent the cancerous growth. Meanwhile, the other Kiss members had to replace Eric Carr as their drummer while he carried on with treatments as the band were in the middle of recording a new album. Anyway, the band were set to record the video for the song *God Gave Rock and Roll to You* and Carr asked to be part of the shoot, the band agreed. By the summer of 1991, Eric Carr had lost his hair due to chemotherapy treatments and his health continued to deteriorate. In late September of 1991, Carr suffered an aneurysm and was rushed to the hospital, then just days later, he suffered a brain haemorrhage. The doctors did all they could, but weeks later and Eric Carr died aged 41 on the 24th of November, 1991. Yet, Carr's death was massively overlooked, cos…

Here in England, the greatest frontman to a band ever also died on the same day. The rumours about Freddie Mercury's health had been questioned by the press for a while, he often looked pale and thin on the rare occasion he made a public appearance. We the public didn't know it at the time, but Mercury had been slowly dying of the AIDS virus. Despite his illness slowly killing him, Freddie Mercury continued to record music with his band, Queen, right up to the end. On the 23rd of November, 1991, Mercury asked the band's manager, Jim Beach, to help prepare a statement for the press and public which said:

"Following the enormous conjecture in the press over the last two weeks, I wish to confirm that I have been tested HIV positive and have AIDS. I felt it correct to keep this information private to date to protect the privacy of those around me. However, the time has come now for my friends and fans around the world to know the truth and I hope that everyone will join with me, my doctors and all those worldwide in the fight against this terrible disease. My privacy has always been very special to me and I am famous for my lack of interviews. Please understand this policy will continue."

Just under twenty-four hours after issuing that statement, and Freddie Mercury died of bronchial pneumonia resulting from the AIDS virus and the world mourned, forgetting all about Eric Carr's death.

19th & 20th OF APRIL 1992

My comedy tastes are perhaps, just as eclectic as my music ones and of course, being British means I grew up on very British humour. Frankie Howerd was one of those comedians I grew up watching back in the eighties and his 'ooooooooooooooooh no missus' and 'titter ye not' catchphrases became part of my lexicon. Howerd was huge in the seventies appearing on TV and in films, he was even part of the famed and very British Carry On film franchise. His *Up Pompeii* TV show and its film spin-off made Frankie Howerd a household name. Though sadly, Howerd struggled with his homosexuality, which he hid from anyone outside of his personal immediate circle, worrying his sexuality could ruin his career. While on a Christmas trip to the Amazon River in 1991, Frankie Howerd contracted a virus. Then, by April of 1992, he began to suffer from respiratory problems. Howerd collapsed at his home and died of heart failure just a few weeks later on the 19th of April, 1992. As with any famous death, the tributes for Frankie Howerd began to pour in and appear in the newspapers. One such tribute was from a close friend and fellow comedian, Benny Hill which said:

"We were great, great friends."

The Benny Hill tribute also mentioned how much he respected Frankie Howerd as a gifted comedian. However, there was a slight problem with that Frankie Howerd obituary that Benny Hill had contributed to.

After it had been revealed that Frankie Howerd had passed away, Benny Hill's agent tried calling him to get a quote as a tribute to the recently dead Howerd. Now, Benny Hill was known to be a bit of a recluse and only spoke to people when he wanted to, so trying to get Hill to talk to anyone was an endeavour at the best of times. Anyway, Hill's agent called and called Hill on the phone for hours with no reply. At the time, the newspapers were asking for tributes for the obituary from Frankie Howerd's friends, so as the agent just couldn't get hold of Hill, he made up the tribute himself. Yes, the Frankie Howerd tribute from Benny Hill wasn't from Hill at all. However, why Benny Hill's agent couldn't get hold of the comedy star was because, Benny Hill himself had died alone in his home, just a few hours after Frankie Howerd had. While Hill's body was not discovered for a few days after, on the 22nd of April, his death was recorded as being on the 20th of April, 1992, the day after Frankie Howerd. Benny Hill died of coronary thrombosis.

31st OF OCTOBER, 1993

Federico Fellini is often celebrated as one of the finest European film-makers ever. If you ever study film, then the work of Fellini is a subject you'd really have to get into, often described as true art over film. Federico Fellini often explored subjects such as dreams, nostalgia and sexuality in his work, to create ground-breaking cinema through the fifties to the nineties, his career spanned five decades and won five Oscars, along with numerous other awards. In June of 1993, Fellini was taken into hospital in Zürich for an angioplasty on his femoral artery, which was a success. However, just two months later and he suffered a stroke and became partially paralysed as a result. He was transferred to a hospital in Rome where he suffered a second stroke that left him in a coma. Then on the 17th of October, Fellini had a heart attack and died later on the 31st of October, 1993. While Europe lost one of its true visionary film-makers, Hollywood lost one of its brightest, young stars too.

River Phoenix had recently finished working on his latest film, *Dark Blood*. Looking for a bit of downtime, Phoenix went to the Viper Room, a very popular nightclub on Sunset Strip, Los Angeles and once owned by Johnny Depp. The club was a known hangout of many a Hollywood star. Phoenix arrived set to play with his alternative rock band... and partake in some drug usage too. Now, accounts on exactly what happened seem to vary from source to source as drugged up Hollywood star rarely make great witnesses. But what is know is that River Phoenix overdosed on (probably) cocaine. After a scuffle in the club, Phoenix was taken outside by security staff, where he collapsed and began having convulsions. His brother, Joaquin, called emergency services (the transcript can be found online, too long to publish here). While his sister, Rain, attempted mouth-to-mouth resuscitation. River Phoenix was rushed to hospital where further attempts to resuscitate him were unsuccessful. Phoenix was pronounced dead at 1:51 AM on the 31st of October, 1993, he was just 23-years-old.

15th & 16th OF FEBRUARY, 1996

M*A*S*H (an acronym for Mobile Army Surgical Hospital) was a popular TV drama-sit-com series set during the Korean War of 1950 - 1953. The show became popular for its funny, but also hard-hitting stories. I mean seriously, look up the finale of the TV show with Hawkeye and the chicken. The show was full of memorable characters, one such character was Lieutenant Colonel Henry Braymore Blake, who was played by McLean Stevenson. At the time, Stevenson was already a popular TV actor and went on to have a successful career in TV and movies even after *M*A*S*H* ended in 1975, one of the highest-rated shows in US television history. McLean Stevenson had been diagnosed with bladder cancer and was recovering in hospital following surgery. But on the 15th of February, 1996, Stevenson suffered a sudden and fatal heart attack.

Now, the TV show *M*A*S*H* was actually a spin-off of the movie version from 1970. Only one cast member from the film *M*A*S*H* went on to also be in the TV show, so everyone else was recast from the film. The character of Lieutenant Colonel Henry Braymore Blake in the movie version was played by Roger Bowen. Coincidentally, Bowen also suffered a sudden heart attack that killed him... and on the 16th of February 1996, only a few hours after McLean Stevenson died. Both actors, who played the same character in the two different versions of *M*A*S*H* died just a few hours apart on different days, and both from heart attacks too. As the deaths were so close together, Roger Bowen's family didn't actually let the news of his passing public until later, as they didn't want to encroach on the death of McLean Stevenson or cause confusion over both actors who had played the same character dying so close together.

27th OF MARCH, 2002

Milton Berle and Billy Wilder where two massive entertainers in their day. Berle was huge on radio and TV. In fact, he soon became known as 'Mr. Television', he was one of the early adaptors of TV coming from a previous stage and radio background in 1929... yes 1929 when Milton Berle took part in an early TV experimental broadcast. But it was in the forties when Berle's TV career really took off. So huge he became that the NBC network offered him a one million dollars a year, thirty-year television contract in 1951. That's just insane, no wonder they called him Mr. Television. Milton Berle final TV role came about in 2000, so he had been on TV in the 1920s through to the year 2000! It was April of 2001 when Berle was diagnosed with a malignant tumour in his colon. As the tumour would take over a decade to become a danger to his health, Berle refused any treatment as he was 92 at the time so saw little point. The following year on the 27th of March, 2002, Milton Berle died from colon cancer.

That same day and famed film director, Billy Wilder also died. Wilder was known for flicks such as *Double Indemnity*, *Sunset Boulevard*, *Some Like It Hot* and *The Apartment* (to name a few). Billy Wilder was a multi-award-winning writer and director who left a legacy of being known for pushing censorship to its very limits in his films. Wilder's films paved the way for future directors to make movies that Hollywood was not exactly welcoming of at the time. Billy Wilder had several health issues later in his life, including cancer, but he died of pneumonia at the age of 95 with a career spanning seven decades. Still, while America Mourned two greats, we Brits were busy saying goodbye to one of our very own legends.

Actor, writer, comedian, musician, and composer, Dudley Moore was an early pioneer of satirical comedy. It was the *Beyond the Fringe* show from 1960 where Moore got his big break and met his future comedy partner Peter Cook. The Pete and Dud characters they created as some of the very finest in British comedy. In the late seventies, Dudley Moore moved to Los Angeles to try to forge a film career. From that, we got classic comedy flicks like: *10* and *Arthur*. Moore had a very successful career on both TV and in movies for decades and became very much loved on both sides of the pond. In 1997, he was diagnosed with calcium deposits in his brain and had suffered irreversible frontal lobe damage. Later that same year and Dudley Moore underwent quadruple heart bypass surgery as well as suffering four strokes. In 1999, Moore announced that he was suffering from a terminal degenerative brain disorder called progressive supranuclear palsy. His health quickly deteriorated and he died on the morning of the 27th of March, 2002 aged 66-years-old. Three true legends of the entertainment world all gone on the same day.

25th OF JUNE, 2009

Farrah Fawcett was a genuine Hollywood hottie. Making a name for herself on TV and in movies through the seventies and eighties and appearing in flicks like *Logan's Run* and *The Cannonball Run*. But perhaps her most famous role was as Jill Munroe in the popular TV show *Charlie's Angels*. While Fawcett really mane a name for herself in the seventies and eighties, she still had a steady career right up to 2009, the year she died. Farrah Fawcett was diagnosed with cancer in 2006 and started treatments to try and beat the terrible disease almost immediately. The chemotherapy and various surgeries worked too, as on the 2nd of February, 2007, Farrah Fawcett's 60th birthday, it was reported that Fawcett was finally cancer-free.

Sadly, that didn't last long as a few months later in May of 2007, Farrah Fawcett was diagnosed with stage IV cancer. Despite several more treatments, Fawcett was hospitalised in April 2009, unconscious and in a critical condition. Though initial reports stated that Fawcett's hospitalisation had nothing to do with cancer, the longer she remained in hospital, the weaker and more ill she became. In early April, Farrah Fawcett was allowed to return home, to spend her final weeks in more conformable surroundings. Then at 9:28 AM on the 25th of June, 2009, Farrah Fawcett died of anal cancer aged 62. As the press were readying their stories and tributes to one of America's most famed and loved faces, someone else died just a few hours later. Someone that pretty much pushed Farrah Fawcett's death to the background.

Paramedics received an emergency call at 12:22 PM regarding a 50-year-old male who had stopped breathing at his home in North Carolwood Drive, Holmby Hills, Los Angeles. That male just so happened to be one of the most famous music icons on the planet, Michael Jackson. Now, I'm not going to get into the whole Jackson death, his personal life, the drugs, Conrad Murray and all that. But, due to the passing of Michael Jackson just a few hours after the death of Farrah Fawcett, the press seemingly forgot all about Fawcett as Jackson made his way to the front of the papers and lead story in the news at the time. Cha-mone!

THANKS

As always, I begin by thanking Louisa, the Mother of my children and my rock during a particularly rough time of my life. Always there for me no matter what, even when I am being an awkward arse.

My children for just being there when Daddy needs a cuddle and a kiss. The reason Daddy stays up till the early hours of the morning tapping away on his laptop, to hopefully give you the best life I can.

Mummy Mo. For everything you've ever done for me and ever will. Your love and support is never-ending and inspiring.

My brothers for being my brothers, blood-related or not.

Auntie Sue. I said in my previous book that you were going to be my good luck charm and I'd include a character in each of my books named after you. Sadly no characters in a factual book, so this mention will have to do instead.

Auntie Chris. You always show an interest when I'm working on a new book and for that I'm grateful. Much more to come too.

The rest of my family and friends for just being there. You know who you are.

Badger Nimahson for buying my books and even giving them a shout out.

And last but not least, anyone who has read this book to this point. Thanks for buying my work and giving me a chance. I hope you enjoyed it and didn't die reading this book or I'd have to include you in a sequel. Also, tell your friends about this and get them to buy a copy.

SOURCES

abc.net.au, abcactionnews.com, abcnews.go.com, agnostilibrary.com,
agraveinterest.blogspot.com, airandspace.si.edu, allthatsinteresting.com,
apnews.com, archive.boston.com, arstechnica.com,
attractionsmanagement.com, atvtoday.co.uk, baltimore.cbslocal.com,
baltimorebrew.com, bostonleadershipbuilders.com, britannica.com,
buzzfeednews.com, capitalpunishmentuk.org, cbsnews.com,
chicago.cbslocal.com, chicago.suntimes.com, china.globaltimes.cn,
cia.gov, coasterbuzz.com, complex.com, connectionnewspapers.com,
culturacolectiva.com, dailyherald.com, dailymail.co.uk,
dailymaverick.co.za, dailymotion.com, darkhistories.com,
darkinthepark.com, darwinawards.com, elitedaily.com,
encyclopediadramatica.rs, esquire.com, eu.floridatoday.com,
factinate.com, findagrave.com, fwi.co.uk, greatadventurehistory.com,
grunge.com, guardian.ng, historic-uk.com, history.com,
historycollection.co, houstonpress.com, huffpost.com, ibtimes.com,
independent.co.uk, infoniagara.com, inquisitr.com,
investigationdiscovery.com, kansascity.com, mentalfloss.com,
mirror.co.uk, murderpedia.org, mydeathspace.com, nbcchicago.com,
nbcnews.com, news.com.au ,news.google.com, news24.com,
newsone.com, newspapers.com, nfpa.org, nypost.com, nytimes.com,
nz.news.yahoo.com, nzherald.co.nz, ocweekly.com, oldbaileyonline.org,
opposingviews.com, people.com, piersmorgan.blogs.cnn.com,
planetdolan.com, pressreader.com, pulse.ng, rawstory.com,
rebelcircus.com, riverfronttimes.com, sandiegoreader.com,
sandiegouniontribune.com, sanfrancisco.cbslocal.com,
smithsonianmag.com, snopes.com, sohopress.com, standard.co.uk,
stuff.co.nz,, taipeitimes.com, tampabay.com, texasmonthly.com,
theclever.com, thedailyrecord.com, theguardian.com, theledger.com,
themeparkinsider.com, themeparkreview.com, theregister.co.uk,
thesmokinggun.com, thestar.com, thesun.co.uk, thevintagenews.com,
trove.nla.gov.au, unbelievable-facts.com, unexplained-mysteries.com,
upi.com, vintagedisneylandtickets.blogspot.com, voice-online.co.uk,
washingtonpost.com, web.archive.org, websleuths.com, weirdnj.com,
wikipedia.org, witn.com, wordandscale.com, woundedtimes.org,
yellowstonepark.com

BOOK OF DEATHS

Printed in Great Britain
by Amazon